GOLDEN YEARS
OF
DUDLEY

The publishers would like to thank the following companies for their

support in the production of this book

The Angle Ring Company Limited

R Bennett & Company Limited

John Buckley (Dudley) Limited

Dudley Building Society

Dudley Borough Council Markets

Dudley College

Computeach International

H & E Knowles (Lye) Limited

Robert Lickley Refractories Limited

William Round (Transport) Limited

First published in Great Britain by True North Books Limited
England HX3 6AE
01422 344344

ISBN 1 903204 60 7

Text, design and origination by True North Books Limited
Printed and bound by The Amadeus Press Limited

GOLDEN YEARS OF DUDLEY

Contents

Introduction

We have all taken to the road on our travels and most of us, at some time, have taken to the air. Others have used the seas around our island, but with 'Dudley Memories' it is an opportunity to indulge in time travel. There is no magical Tardis to transport you back through history, just page after page of pure nostalgia. Wonderful images, all carefully captioned with informative and pithy text, will help the reader return to the last century without ever leaving the armchair in which he is sitting. As you turn each leaf you will be able to share those days when dad was a lad or grandma did the jitterbug. Our towns and boroughs have changed so much since their times that it is hard to bring to mind just how everything used to be. Thank goodness for the camera, for without a pictorial record so much of our recent history would be a mere memory. You know how unreliable unsupported reminiscences can be as the mind can play tricks. But, the camera never lies and all the pictures and photographs are accompanied by words that

sharpen the recollections you might have. The reader will have personal experience of some of the scenes, while others will be brought to mind by the stories our parents and grandparents told us. In this book you will be able to see what it was they were talking about when referring to certain streets and events. There are other photographs and memory joggers that you will be able to remember for yourself. Perhaps this book might even settle a wager or two. Quite often people remember the same occasion or place in different ways. If there is a fact or picture in this book that helps you win the bet, then good luck. However if it was your memory that was playing tricks, then you can always turn to the next page! There will be plenty more of interest to follow.

'Dudley Memories' is not intended to be a dry and dusty old history book. It is meant to be a means for the reader to indulge in a wave of nostalgia for a century that is not too far behind us, but is growing more distant with each passing day. The 20th century brought us so much. The aeroplane flew for

Boy scouts getting to grips with car cleaning during Bob-a-job Week in 1951.

the first time, electrical appliances changed the way we ran our households and entertained ourselves, women were liberated and the country became a multicultural society. Villages grew into towns, industry replaced agriculture as our setting and new and ever wider roads swept away the lanes and cottages of our heritage. Little shops became supermarkets, tower blocks rose on the skyline and the computer chip replaced the brain. Without pictorial records of the past we would only be able to rely on the written or spoken word for our nostalgia. But, with 'Dudley Memories' there is a chance to claw back those days of yesteryear. Sit your children down and leaf through the book with them for, although they are our future, they must not be allowed to ignore their heritage. Make sure that they have cameras of their own so that they can repeat the process for generations to come and present them with an opportunity to learn from our mistakes and build upon our successes. Nostalgia does not mean that you are wallowing in the past, but remembering the good times and shedding a silent tear for when it was less so. Not everything in your background is wonderful, but it would be a crime to be unable to preserve those bits that were.

The basis for modern Dudley is in Anglo Saxon times, though evidence of man settling in the vicinity goes back some 10,000 years. However, it was with the Saxon lord Duddah and 'Duddah's leah', the woodland clearing in which he lived, that we can clearly see the derivation of the name by which our town is known today. He built a wooden castle on the site of the present one at the beginning of the eighth century AD and from a small initial community there grew a settlement of significant proportions. An important market was established in Dudley c1260 and at about the same time valuable deposits of clay, iron ore and coal were discovered. These gave rise to the small industries that grew up and included pits, mines and forges long before the words 'industrial revolution' were invented. Wood and charcoal

continued to be the major fuels, but forests were rapidly shrinking as demand increased as the population grew. Dud Dudley (1599-1684), son of Edward Sutton, 5th Baron Dudley, began to experiment with alternative fuels in his family ironworks. He smelted iron ore with coke or, as he called it, 'pit-coal', a hard mass of almost pure carbon made from bituminous coal. Dudley obtained a patent for his innovation in 1621 and was soon producing a record seven tons of pig iron per week at the Hasco Bridge

Christmas in Market Place, 1950.

ironworks. The tremendous expansion of industry after 1700 was stimulated by the building of canals that transformed the communications of the area. By the first half of the 19th century there were numerous blast furnaces whose pollution helped to give the Black Country its name. Nail making was an important domestic industry and chains and anchors were also made. Glassmaking dates from the early 17th century, and crystal glassware is produced today. Metalworking remains an important industry of the district with products ranging from heavy engineering castings to tubes, chains, cables, nuts, and bolts. Other industries include plastics, textiles, chemicals, and electronics, but these latter developments bring us closer to the present than this book intends to be.

The focus of the following pages will be clearly placed in the middle years of the last century when boys went to war and came back as men, Ford Populars drove through the town centre and girls swooned at the handsome face of James Dean on the movie screen. Return to Wolverhampton Street when beer was sold at the Crown for one and six a pint or shop at the market where carrots were weighed in pounds and ounces without fear of prosecution. Hop aboard a trolley bus and take a ride along Hall Street before the Southern Bypass cut underneath it and yodel Frank Ifield's 'I Remember You' as the journey unfolds. It is now time to step out of your personal Tardis and take to the pages and images that will make you long for days that can never be revisited in the flesh, but this is a good second best. Think how it was to play board games with the children once more when they had tired of hopscotch, marbles, conkers and jacks. Pull up a chair and put another lump of coal on the fire. That should help rekindle the nostalgic mood. Reach for a glass of dandelion and burdock, filled from a stone jar, and pick up a penny Arrow bar to chew on. Light up a Craven A, 'for your throat's sake', and smooth down your sack dress or slick your hair back with Brilliantine. Wind up the gramophone, put a new needle into the stylus and let Nat 'King' Cole soothe you with 'Mona Lisa'. Older readers can toss a farthing to decide who can turn the first page. The lucky winner is about to begin a journey to a Dudley that we should never forget. It is our heritage; something to be proud of as it helped make each and every one of us the people we are today.

Street scenes

Left: St Edmund's Church provided a good platform from which to take this elevated photograph looking from the end of Castle Street towards the entrance gates that mark the driveway leading up to Dudley Castle. The main buildings in view are still with us, with the one on the left now The Fellows, a Beefeater pub and restaurant. The cottages on the right are now a nice historic touch behind the 20th century traffic lights of The Broadway and Castle Hill. Lord Ednam leased the castle grounds to the council in 1924 for use as a public park at the generously low rate of 10s (50p) per annum. However, that arrangement was abandoned in 1932 after a series of political arguments and disagreements between the owner and the local government. Relationships were not improved by attempts to replace the castle flagpole with the mast of the 'Britannia'. Thankfully, civil war did not break out over the matter because no one wanted a repetition of the events of the 1640s when the castle was bombarded, besieged and eventually partly demolished by order of Parliament. The opening of the zoo in 1937, just before the second world war rekindled interest in the grounds and restoration work to the castle in the latter years of the last century culminated with the completion of the visitor centre in 1994.

Above: This was Stone Street before it was widened and its shops replaced by more up to date ones and the modernised Fountain Arcade. The advertisers on the gable end did not want you to go down there anyway, suggesting that you would be better served by a visit to Westley's garage on Castle Hill for a replacement car or a stroll around the corner to New Street where Betteridge could provide lovers with a wide choice of wedding rings. The company said that it had some that were the latest shape, a statement that caused a few to scratch their heads and wonder what that meant. How a ring could be anything other than round was a puzzle that could only be solved by a visit to Betteridge's private room. On 30 March 1938 the group of men lounging on the corner had other things to occupy their minds. Motor cars were for toffs and pretty rings for those who were well heeled. Although unemployment was not as high as it had been earlier in the decade, jobs were not guaranteed and, for the working man, his wage packet never contained enough to allow him to entertain dreams of the open road with baubles adorning his wife's fingers. There were also rumblings across Europe that might just come to occupy his mind in the next few years.

Above: Underneath a stormy sky a man on crutches makes his way carefully across Tower Street in the mid 1950s. Did he lose his leg a decade or so ago in defence of his country? War memorials help us remember the ultimate sacrifice paid by our heroes, but there were thousands of others who did return from those foreign fields with shattered bodies and damaged minds to discover that they were expected to pick up the reins of their lives with little concrete assistance from the powers that be. The little group on the pavement was outside the Court House, across the way from the police station. There has been a police presence in the town since 1840 when the force was part of the Worcestershire Constabulary. Dudley's own service was not established until 1920. Further down the road we can still see the building that first housed the fire service in 1941. Dudley had a fire brigade as long ago as 1834, though the town was mainly serviced by insurance brigades in early Victorian times. The first town fire engine was purchased in 1871 when the police provided the personnel and a fire station was established on Priory Street in 1892. That building became a shoe repair shop and then a café after the move to Tower Street. As the 20th century drew to a close the congestion around the town centre caused increasing problems for the fire appliances to function swiftly and safely. Some £500,000 was also needed to give the fire station a face lift, so it was sensible to draw a line under the old building's service and make the move to Burton Road, as the service did in April 1999 at a cost of £2.3 million.

Below: The puzzled look on the man's face as he emerges from the Gents seems to be directed at the woman in front of him. Surely she had not paid a visit to the wrong department? Spending a penny was easier in 1956 as public toilets were commonplace in our town centres. Descending the steps into some dungeon and being faced with solid doors and their penny slot mechanisms and sliding brass knobs was like entering a troglodyte's den. Council cuts and vandalism took away many of these conveniences, leaving those with a desperate need to pretend to be interested in the array of St Michael vests in M & S whilst casting an eye across the store for a picture or silhouette of the appropriate gender. Had the man been photographed alone it might have been hard to identify the era of this shot if you relied upon his dress sense. However, the woman's clothing is a giveaway. The large bag would have been stuffed with a purse, brush, handkerchief, keys, Co-op divvy card, return bus ticket, scissors, library tickets and all manner of other personal items, but just leaving enough room for a little shopping from the market. The hat firmly plonked upon her head was the symbol of a lady. No self respecting woman was properly dressed without a head covering and a headscarf was for a younger generation, even if the Queen had been known to wear one.

How gentle was the scene on Tower Street in 1957 as we look down the hill from the Court House Inn towards The Broadway that was officially opened in May 1935 as a bypass from Castle Hill to Burton Road. The impressive castle, rising in the distance above the trees, was no longer the seat of power and authority that it had once been, but remained a symbol of the medieval days when the lords of Dudley had the temerity to challenge the monarchy or when John Dudley became Duke of Northumberland. In the 17th century the castle was bombarded from Kate's Hill during the Civil War, after which it ceased to have any great military significance. Latterly its function was largely ceremonial, hosting various festivals and fetes, but it lives on as a tourist attraction and is fondly regarded by locals as a piece of Dudley's great history, demonstrating that this part of the Black Country has more to its roots than coal and iron ore. The sleepy view of Tower Street lets today's generation appreciate that it was not all that long ago when hustle and bustle was far from the norm. Strangers greeted each other in the street and friends stopped for a chat as there was nothing pressing them that could be delayed for five minutes while a conversation was completed.

Left: The war memorial tower is linked into the town hall offices that can be entered via this gateway that looks out along Stone Street. Through it the camera was opening a window onto the world as it stood in 1957: A time when we were starting to turn the corner from the austerity of the immediate postwar years that would lead us into the Harold Macmillan 'never had it so good' era. Families were beginning to regard the motor car as an item that was universally affordable, rather than just the province of the middle classes. Televisions appeared in the corners of living rooms, pushing the wireless into the background. Housewives put away their dolly tubs and mangles and went for washing machines and spin dryers as the treadled sewing machine was replaced by one that plugged into the wall. Macmillan replaced the sick Anthony Eden in January, despite the fact that Rab Butler had been favourite to take over, and he guided the country into a new age with such success that cartoonists dubbed him 'Supermac'. It had been another Tory prime minister, Bewdley born Stanley Baldwin, who officiated at the opening ceremony of Dudley's memorial tower on 16 October 1928 in honour of those who had fallen in the Great War.

Above: The Old Meeting House is not far from where Wolverhampton Street enters Market Place. Entrance is made to the old Unitarian church, established in 1701-02, through the archway next to Payne's shoe and stocking repair shop that was about to move to premises on the opposite Priory Street in 1959. In the 21st century of disposable goods, many people still use a shoe repairer. But repairs for stockings? At 22 Wolverhampton Street B & D Typewriter Services, a company that also had outlets in Birmingham and Manchester, catered for all office needs, including Smith-Corona and Underwood typewriters, adding machines, carbon paper, special erasers and correction fluid. How different the office of yesterday was in comparison with the one we now have and its calculators, word processing packages, graphics suites, broadband internet connections and department heads who turn up for work in jeans and open necked shirts and are known by their Christian names. It is no longer a requirement that a secretary can rattle off her Pitman shorthand at 120 words per minute, a skill earned at night school or day release at the local college where book keeping and accounting were also part of the course-work. Today's boss clicks his fingers and, in response, the secretary just clicks her mouse.

Above: Tower Street runs from The Broadway down to Stone Street, crossing New Street on its way. The photographer stood at this crossroads in 1958 from a spot in between the police station and the Court House Inn, once called the Court House Tavern and occasionally used as a court house for local cases, so providing the background for the pub's name. The old jail and workhouse stood near here on what was formerly known as Pease Lane. Looking down to Stone Street the Morris Minor on the right is the epitome of British car manufacture in its heyday, now a thing of the past. Designed by Alec Issigonis, who went on to develop the BMC Mini, this car remained in production from 1948 to 1971. Noted for its reliability and excellent steering and cornering qualities, the Morris Minor was the first all-British model to pass the one million mark in sales. Surviving models are still cherished by owners and collectors. It was something to be noted in the diary if any foreign import was spotted on our streets in 1958. British cars had such delightfully domestic

sounding names with the Morris Cowley, Austin Cambridge and Standard Vanguard. Nearly half a century on we have become used to flashier titles like Primera, Toledo and Vectra, but there was something cosier about a Hillman Imp or a Riley Elf.

Far left: Although the Empire's name still stood out in relief on the front of the building on Hall Street in 1959 it had long ceased to be an important name in the Dudley entertainment scene. It had been introduced to the town as a palace of varieties, promising something more than a music hall, on 6 May 1903. Dan Leno, the country's top entertainer, topped the bill on opening night. His wistful and comic caricatures endeared him to audiences and he was the first music hall act to be invited to be part of the Royal Command Performance when he appeared in front of Edward VII. The theatre, designed by local architect Arthur Gammage, catered for a massive audience of 2,000. Its partially sliding roof providing ventilation and relief from patrons' tobacco smoke. The Empire became a full time cinema on 8 January 1912, having shared duties as a theatre and picture house for several years, and flourished in the 1920s. Children's Saturday matinees were introduced early in that decade and for those who could not afford the penny admission there was always the chance to peek through the gap in the big exit doors. It closed on 2

November 1940 after a showing of George Formby's 'Let George do it' and became a wartime factory and warehouse. In peacetime Herman Smith's engineering company used the premises before they were demolished and the site taken over by a supermarket.

Top: Cars were built for the purpose of getting from A to B and it is only since the 1960s that manufacturers have attempted to woo customers with bright colours rather than the uniform black that Henry Ford once told us was the shade we could expect from his production line. The colour of mourning might have seemed appropriate on the vehicles in Upper Hall Street in 1958 as everywhere in Dudley was still trying to come to terms with the loss of one of its favourite sons. On 6 February a dreadful plane crash in Munich had robbed the world of eight of Manchester United's Busby Babes and among them was the 21 year old Duncan Edwards, one of Dudley's own. He had already won a string of England caps and was destined to be the greatest player this country has ever produced, but his flower blossomed so briefly. One of the few bright spots to lighten the mood was provided by the Guinness advert. The company has always had an eye and an ear for an interesting picture or a witty slogan. Visitors to Dudley Zoo on spotting a toucan do not think of the bird's natural habitat in the Amazon jungle or across the Andes, but immediately conjure up an image on a hoarding of the brightly plumed creature and a foaming glass of the black stuff. As recent adverts would have it, now that is pure genius.

Both pictures: Here are two views taken from virtually the same spot, though separated from one another in time by a matter of just a year or two in the early 1960s. High Side (centre), on the northern side of High Street, was an elevated section above the carriageway with Greystone Street running behind it. The old terraced property was ripe for demolition and, even if there had been any objections, these would have been swept away by the evidence supplied by the white house. Severe subsidence had affected its stability and its removal would have been required just on safety grounds alone. The houses were photographed looking down the A4101 towards Queen's Cross from close to the junction of High Street and King Street. The 1960s were a time of regeneration as housing stocks were upgraded, continuing the process of the postwar years, and attention given to improving facilities and traffic flow in and around Dudley town centre. When the buildings on High Side were demolished the council gave some thought to the aesthetic lines that a visitor coming from the direction of Kingswinford or Brierley Hill might encounter. First impressions, heading towards St Thomas's Church after about 1964, must

have been favourable because the neatly landscaped grass and flowerbeds were a vast improvement on the dilapidated housing that had been there. Today, this side of the road is still pretty to look at, though the view has changed in character. Trees and bushes that were planted nearly 40 years ago have now reached maturity and form a pleasant green barrier to the developments behind. The shops and retail outlets on the south side of the road, however, are now starting to look their age, though they are still very recognisable as the buildings we can see here, but have changed significantly in character in the interim. Where once we had Dartmouth Garage, Castle Electrics and the others those same buildings now house Derann AV, Chutney Mary, the Halal Meat Centre and the Rajput and Kashmir jewellers. These modern names illustrate the changing face of Dudley as it has become a more cosmopolitan town, populated by a more diverse people who include Bengali, Gujerati, Urdu and Pushto among their first languages. The changing face of the town is not limited to the nature of its shops for there is also a large mosque and community centre on the corner of Birmingham Street and Castle Hill.

Below: On the right, Nipper and his gramophone loudspeaker were advertising His Master's Voice records on 78 rpm. The American Alfredo Cocozza was one of the company's top artists and his glorious voice soared into the charts with 'I'll walk with God' in 1955, though we all remember him by the stage name of Mario Lanza. Teenagers, though, were turning towards the Brunswick label where a dumpy 30-year old called Bill Haley was rocking around the clock. The main shop frontage belonged to Timothy White's and Taylor's, a major rival to Boot's as a chemist and dispenser of cosmetic products. Many a little lad went inside its doors just before Christmas to buy his mum some smellies or bath salts for her present. On the big day she kissed him and thanked him for his kind thoughtfulness and carefully put the presentation box into the bathroom cabinet, next to the identical one he had got her for her birthday. Look along Stone Street from the junction with Market Place today and the scene is very much the same. The corner is still dominated by the rectangular tower of the Brooke Robinson Museum and council offices, though the museum that opened in 1931 closed in the mid 1960s and its contents moved to the art gallery on Priory Street. Town Hall departments have now taken over the rooms that were named for the man who served as Conservative MP for 20 years after his election in 1886.

The two elderly ladies walking along Stone Street in 1960 had witnessed such great changes in life style since the Victorian days of their birth. Electricity had come to light their way and gas was on tap in every home to provide the power for their cookers and living room fires. Motor cars and lorries had replaced four legged transport and the welfare state was providing some comforts in their old age. Satellites orbited the earth and aeroplanes circled overhead. They had even been able to replace some inventions with others, as when they traded in 'The Archers' on radio for 'Coronation Street' on television. Their tram cables had been

superseded by ones used by trolley buses and, as the wires buzzed above them, the couple discussed how their shops had changed beyond recognition. The ladies were heading for the Fountain Arcade, that brainchild of Alderman TW Tanfield, a resident of Tower Street who ran the Fountain Stationery Company. He contracted architect George Coslett and builders Crump and Round to produce an arcade with an attractive glass roof and prettily patterned mosaic floor. His wife performed the opening ceremony in 1926 and let us hope that the old ladies were still around to see the modernisation that took place towards the end of the 60s.

It is not just the perspective of the photograph that makes Wolverhampton Street appear to get narrower as it trails away from Priory Street towards the corner of Market Place because it actually gets quite claustrophobic the nearer a pedestrian gets to that point. Despite that it has long been one of Dudley's main roads, dating back to when it was Smythe Lane in the 14th century. As a turnpike road it had a large number of hotels, taverns, beerhouses and inns dotted along its length. One of these, the Crown at 201 Wolverhampton Street, on the corner of Priory Street, dates from 1819 when it was known as the Coach and Horses, an obvious connection with the days when carriages thundered the road as coachmen whipped their steeds into action. The hotel was rebuilt towards the end of the 19th century, reopening under a new name in 1898 as though to finally admit that the great days of coach travel had long been buried by the steam power of the railways. In 1960 it stood opposite the old post office, built in 1879 and enlarged in 1911, that did service until business was transferred to High Street in the mid 1980s. The Crown was once home to Sid Bowser, the old WBA soccer player.

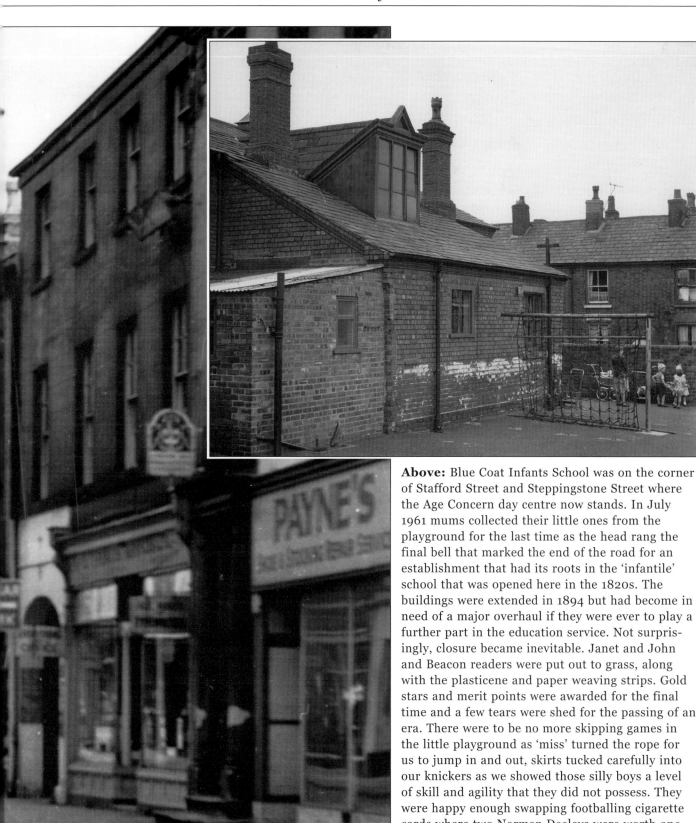

Above: Blue Coat Infants School was on the corner of Stafford Street and Steppingstone Street where the Age Concern day centre now stands. In July 1961 mums collected their little ones from the playground for the last time as the head rang the final bell that marked the end of the road for an establishment that had its roots in the 'infantile' school that was opened here in the 1820s. The buildings were extended in 1894 but had become in need of a major overhaul if they were ever to play a further part in the education service. Not surprisingly, closure became inevitable. Janet and John and Beacon readers were put out to grass, along with the plasticene and paper weaving strips. Gold stars and merit points were awarded for the final time and a few tears were shed for the passing of an era. There were to be no more skipping games in the little playground as 'miss' turned the rope for us to jump in and out, skirts tucked carefully into our knickers as we showed those silly boys a level of skill and agility that they did not possess. They were happy enough swapping footballing cigarette cards where two Norman Deeleys were worth one Derek Kevan. Nor would there be any more broken skulls caused by tumbles from the scrambling net. Imagine the high time today's health and safety executive would have with this piece of equipment and its landing area.

Events & occasions

The boy sitting above the spiked railings might have had a wonderful view of the procession that was setting off from near St Thomas's Church, but it was rather a precarious perch. He will now be in his mid 70s and will shudder at the chances he took as a youngster if he can review the occasion on 6 May 1935 when he watched the silver jubilee celebrations that were mounted in honour of King George V. This was to be the first of a number of events that put the Royal Family onto the front pages of the newspapers in the space of just two years. The rejoicing for King George and Queen Mary, the latter wearing her trademark toque, brought crowds onto the streets in numbers that had not been seen since the end of World War One. However, the nation was united once more in its grief when the King passed away at the beginning of the following year. There then followed the most torrid time the British monarchy had faced for centuries. Edward VIII succeeded his father, but by the end of the year had abdicated when the establishment refused to accept his liaison with the twice divorced American socialite, Wallis Simpson. His brother accepted the crown and, on 12 May 1937, the crowds were back on the streets to welcome George VI to the throne and usher in a period of much needed stability for the residents of Buckingham Palace.

Above: These proud men of the 5th Worcestershire Home Guard paraded with their heads held high as they marched to the beat of the regimental band in 1943. Over 500 registered in Dudley in the first week of its creation. When it was first decided to form an army, originally called Local Defence Volunteers (LDV) and drawn mainly from the ranks of those over 40s who were considered too old to join up in the armed forces, those who came forward were the objects of some scorn. Poorly equipped, they often had to drill with broomsticks and shovels instead of rifles. Cynics said that they were playing at being soldiers and doubted the value that they would have if ever the enemy invaded. Winston Churchill helped change attitudes.

First of all the prime minister renamed the LDV as the Home Guard in the summer of 1941. Idiotic ideas such as launching petrol bombs by catapult or stretching piano wire across a road to decapitate a German motorcyclist were abandoned. Proper weapons and uniforms were issued and training became professionally conducted. The Home Guard became increasingly effective, watching over key installations, releasing regular units for active duties and demonstrating the true value of local knowledge on manoeuvres. Dudley's force performed with distinction until it was stood down in December 1944 at a ceremony in St Thomas's Church. Over 3,500 had enrolled in its ranks at some stage during the war.

Below centre: Out came the best homburgs and toppers to celebrate the opening of Dudley Zoo on 6 May 1937. Looking across the sealion pool Mr AE Marsh and the Earl of Dudley, owner of the castle and its grounds, held centre stage in front of the other worthies who puffed on their cigars and checked the time on hunters located in waistcoat pockets waiting for the official declaration that the grounds were open for business. As co-founders of Dudley Zoological Society it was fitting that this duo should have the honour of cutting the ceremonial ribbon, even if the zoo was not quite finished. Rather than wait for every nut and bolt to be put in place it had been decided to admit the general public in time for the lucrative Whitsuntide trade and as a means of honouring George VI whose coronation was due to be held just six days later. Three peacocks donated by the Duke of Sutherland were the first creatures to make their home here, but the main stocks came from Oxford Zoo where the new manager, Frank Cooper, had been in charge before his appointment in Dudley. By the time the zoo was up and fully running it had over 1,000 animals representing 60 species of mammal and 100 different breeds of feathered friend.

Bottom: Wearing a snake like some Hawaiian garland, Peter Markham Scott performed the opening ceremony at Dudley Zoo's new reptile house on 20 May 1956. Thousands visited the zoo every week, enjoying the sight of the modern architecture and limestone animal pits that were set against the backdrop of the ancient castle keep. It is doubtful if many of them would have had Scott's courage in wrapping a snake around his neck, but he had a particular advantage as he was steeped in animal lore, though birds were his individual forte. Born in 1909, the son of explorer Robert Falcon Scott, he was a renowned painter and sailor. In 1946 he founded the Slimbridge Refuge, a waterfowl sanctuary on the River Severn in Gloucestershire, where through a captive breeding program he saved the Hawaiian goose, or nene, from extinction in the 1950s. Scott guided the World Wildlife Fund as chairman from 1961 to 1982. He presented several wildlife programmes on television and followed in his father's footsteps when he mounted a number of expeditions to Antarctica. Scott received a knighthood in 1973 and died a few months before his 80th birthday. His conservation work will act as a permanent tribute to a man who was tireless in seeking to promote animal welfare.

Left: Britain has had its fair share of comedy double acts who have been popular since the war and each has had a particular era when it was top of any variety bill. The modern Chuckle Brothers are just an extension of the acts of previous decades that brought us Cannon and Ball, Little and Large, Hope and Keen, Mike and Bernie Winters, Denis Goodwin and Bob Monkhouse and, best of all, Morecambe and Wise. But, in the early 1950s, before even Eric and Ernie had become household names, pride of place went to Jimmy Jewel and Ben Warris. There was always a straight man in the duo and it was Ben, on the left, who was the foil for Jimmy's flat capped humour. They were cousins from Sheffield who teamed up in 1934 and formed a double act that was to make them the highest paid turn of its type in the 1950s. By the time they broke up in the mid 60s they had appeared in seven Royal Variety performances. Jimmy went on to appear in TV sitcoms and forged an amusing partnership with Hylda Baker. In 1954 they were helping Sally Barnes christen the zebras at the zoo. It was always good copy for a publicity stunt to make sure that there was a pretty girl on hand and this blonde lovely was just the ticket. Geraldo, the famous bandleader, is on the right. It was said that his band swung better than Ted Heath's. He went on to become involved with band management, supplying acts for the Cunard Liners.

Below: Postwar recovery at Dudley Zoo was helped by the appointment of the new general manager, Donald Bowles, a graduate from Bristol University. Animal numbers had fallen during the war years and he helped build them back up once more and organised further development of the grounds before moving on to a post with Edinburgh Zoo. As one of the ways of raising the profile of the zoo various publicity stunts were arranged. This one involved Harry Hatch, the head keeper, using a novel form of transport to take him to the polling booth in October 1951. Labour had retained power in February 1950, but with a vastly reduced majority compared with its landslide success in 1945. The nation was happy with the welfare state that the government had ushered in but the cost was too dear for many to stomach. Economic mismanagement, devaluation of the pound, slow recovery after the war and no obvious rise in the standard of living had turned many away from continuing to pledge their support for Clement Attlee. His party limped on in power for another 18 months before Harry Hatch and fellow voters turned back to the Conservatives for their salvation. The 77 year old Winston Churchill came back to power, cigar firmly clenched between his teeth, though we are not completely sure where the camel placed his cross on the ballot paper.

Above: There are wars, terrorism and conflicts fuelled by religious differences and bigotry, but everyone loves the Salvation Army. The organisation just does not have an axe to grind, contenting itself with the plight of others and offering support to the needy. When the girl from the Sally Army comes into the roughest and toughest of back street pubs selling the 'War Cry' she is afforded the greatest respect and hard bitten drinkers gladly put a few coppers in her collecting tin. Woe betide anyone who curses even mildly in her presence because his companions will round on him. It was not always so as the organisation founded by William Booth had its meetings disrupted by violent protestors in the early days and, in the 1880s, his followers were subjected to fines and imprisonment as breakers of the peace. All that had long gone by Christmas Eve 1956 as the brass band played carols for those shopping for last minute presents in the town centre. From there the musicians moved off to serenade residents in the outlying streets, setting up on one corner as an officer moved from house to house collecting donations. Occasionally, the spirit of Christmas was thrown into question as when the band struck up 'God rest ye merry gentlemen' in Grange Road. One irate mum bellowed, 'I wish ye merry gentlemen would give it a rest, I've just got the kids off to sleep!'

Right: Battles have been fought, exhibits stolen and vegetables sabotaged all in the interests of winning first prize at the local show. But we must hastily point out that such allegations had never even been dreamt of when the Springfield Working Men's Club was involved. Proudly showing off their onions and leeks on 10 October 1958 their conduct was beyond reproach. Displays of giant chrysanthemums and neatly arranged groups of runner beans on plates are regular prize winners at any show and the culmination of hours spent sowing, hoeing and nurturing delicate seedlings into full bloom on allotments and in greenhouses. The British love of gardening is steeped in our rural heritage, but is also rooted in necessity. When money was scarce families eked out their meagre budgets by growing their own produce and local councils helped the trend by providing land at a knock down rent that could be cultivated by individuals and provide supplements to the cooking pot. During the second world war 'Dig for victory' was one of the main slogans used by the government to encourage us all to use every square yard we could find to bolster the nation's resources. The enjoyment of home grown, fresh fruit and vegetables is even more special in this day and age as our taste buds have been blighted by the mass produced, plastic packaged stuff the supermarkets now foist on us.

Below: It would appear that the statue of the first Earl of Dudley was inspecting the ranks of these young cadets in April 1957 as he stared at the line-up from his elevated dais outside the castle gateway. The noble lord had been here since 1888, but had originally been set to look away from the castle. Wear and tear on his features from erosion determined a complete about face in 1939 when he was turned through 180 degrees to his present position. The parade was really waiting for the Queen to appear during her visit to the town and these lads had spent all morning getting themselves ready for the honour of seeing Her Majesty close up in the flesh. One of the youngsters was still in short trousers and how he must have longed for the day when his mother took him to the outfitter's and bought him his first pair of 'longs'. It was not easy to chat up your first prospective girlfriend if your knees were glinting in the sun and your socks had wrinkles in them that would rival those of Norah Batty. However jaunty an angle you wore your cap it could not disguise the fact that mum did not think that you were big enough just yet.

Right: Dudley's Mayor, Councillor S Danks, had donned every conceivable ceremonial robe that he could muster on 23 April 1957 when Her Majesty called in during her whistle stop tour of 11 midlands' towns. The Queen and her entourage drove past cheering crowds lining Birmingham Road, Castle Hill and the Broadway before arriving in the centre for a walkabout near the Council House. The building, designed by Harvey,

opened in 1935 but had seen no more exalted visitor pass its doors than the elegant, but simply clad, monarch who graced Dudley on that fine spring day. Although wearing the gloves that ladies of a certain rank always wore in public, whatever the temperature, the rest of her outfit marked a less formal attitude that helped her subjects feel that she was more in touch with them than some of her predecessors had been. Her more modern approach indicated a style better suited to the second half of the 20th century as the general public began to lose its awe of the monarchy, whilst still maintaining a mixture of respect and affection. The nation had taken the young woman to its heart when she was thrust into the limelight as a 25 year old on the sudden death of her father, George VI, in 1952. During her time in Dudley she was presented with numerous bouquets and also accepted locally produced leather goods in a presentation made in the Town Hall.

Far right: On 21 November 1962 Princess Margaret officially opened a £400,000 extension to Dudley Training College, but also took time out to visit St Thomas's Church where she was photographed being greeted by the Vicar, Canon and Mrs Keith Murray. A vivacious woman, she was a handsomely attractive personality in those days and a far

cry from the ill, worn out figure she became in the last years of her life that ended in February 2002. As a young woman she had performed some official duties, but her work became even more important and her life much busier once her sister had acceded to the throne in 1952. Born on 21 August 1930 Princess Margaret Rose was but a slip of a young woman when she visited Dudley, yet it was obvious from the admiring glances she drew that here was a beauty who could turn heads. She was something of a rebellious and forthright person, as second children often are, and soon made her way into the gossip columns of national newspapers with her comments and social whirl. It was her affair with Group Captain Peter Townsend that was to move her onto the front pages in 1955 when it seemed certain that she was going to announce marriage to her father's former equerry. He was a divorced man and the establishment feared ructions that might rival the 1936 abdication crisis. Princess Margaret eventually gave in to the pressure and severed connections with Townsend, but was never to find lasting happiness.

Below: The parade stretched along High Street as far as the eye could see. When the Worcester Diocesan Missionary procession was mounted in 1962 it was a remarkable public display of faith as cassocks and surplices fluttered in the breeze in front of a crowd of fascinated onlookers. It was not that unusual to see such a march, but it more usually happened at Whitsuntide when the members of various church groups paraded across the town in their best clothes. By the 1960s churchgoing had started to lose favour as a traditional way of spending a Sunday morning. Priests and vicars spoke out from their pulpits in an attempt to rally their flocks, but congregations were beginning to be dominated by those with grey hair and thinning locks. Trendy clerics picked up guitars and folksy hymns were written in attempt to persuade the youth of Britain that religion was not just for fuddy-duddies. Curates roared around on motorbikes and grew their hair over their dog collars, but the effect was minimal and the coins in the collecting plates became fewer as each year passed. Despite the fall off another much later march in 1979 drew a large following when Dudley's seven Anglican churches mounted a similarly impressive display of unity in recognition of group ministry.

Right: June 1963 was part of a glorious summer when it seemed that the sun shone brightly enough to persuade many holidaymakers that taking one of those newfangled package trips to Spain was not essential to procuring a tan. High Street was the scene on this day for the Training College to take over centre stage. Looking along the road from St Thomas's towards Market Place there was a line of lorries all decked out as floats that were part of the students' Rag Day. Each tableau had its own particular theme, with the literary and debating society leading the way. Others included the camera club's 'Watch the birdie', one about 'Restoration Dudley' and another proposing a 'Brave new world'. That last one seemed to have some form of demented chicken or drunken ostrich on board, but no doubt the students knew what the relevance was. Young men and women ran along the pavement demanding donations from passers-by or sold them their rag magazines that contained a string of puerile jokes, but included the occasional one that made grandma blush. Elsewhere, dignitaries were kidnapped for ransom, but the whole day's events were all in a good cause. Although some of the students' antics could be irritating, their hearts were in the right place and a healthy sum of money was raised for charity.

At leisure

Put your backs into it lads and heave away with a will. Sports day at Dudley Grammar School on 26 May 1951 was like many others up and down the country where children, allocated to teams or 'houses', competed in traditional athletics events such as this one. Tug of war had even been an Olympic sport early in the 20th century, usually dominated by British police teams. London hosted the 1948 Olympics, referred to as the 'austerity games', but we failed to win anything and it was Emil Zatopek and Fanny Blankers-Koen who were the stars of the show. Our playing fields helped to provide a breeding ground for more success in the 1950s as Chris Brasher, Chris Chataway, Roger Bannister, Gordon Pirie, Derek Ibbotson, Dorothy Shirley, Thelma Hopkins and Dorothy Hyman all came to the fore. None of the Dudley tug of war team went on to smash national records, but they pulled as hard for their side as any prospective medal winner. Dudley Grammar School was steeped in history, right back to its founding date in 1562. From 1899 pupils attended the buildings on St James's Road and when the school amalgamated with two others in 1989 it was renamed Castle High School.

August Bank Holiday Monday in 1957 was delightfully bright and sunny and crowds flocked to the seaside on charas and excursion trains. Those who stayed at home crowded into Dudley Zoo in hordes, as they had been doing for 20 years. On examining their programmes they would have discovered a map that guided them around the various animal pits, houses, pools and enclosures. However, the official guide was not quite as good value for money as it had once been. Just before the war sixpence would have bought a 100 page booklet of which two thirds was packed with information and photographs of a griffon vulture, the oiling of an elephant's hide or a sacred baboon with its cheek pouches stuffed with food. By the time these little girls climbed aboard the camel the publication had halved in size and doubled in price. But that was a minor grumble compared to the scale of the fun that could be had on such a day and it took all morning and afternoon to pack everything in. As well as the enjoyment to be had riding on the camel older readers might recall bouncing along on three tons of Meena or Ranee, two elephants that were popular attractions in the immediate postwar years.

Above: This young man had found a comfortable niche to enjoy his drink on a stick, as one brand of ice lollies was known in 1957. He will now be well into his 50s and perhaps enjoying early retirement and celebrating the fact with a drink that has a twizzle stick in it. He can remember those days of his childhood when little lads had short trousers, long socks and knees that were permanently scabbed from playground tumbles during a 30 a side soccer match with a frayed tennis ball during morning break. When the teacher blew the whistle for a return to lessons it was only half time as the game could carry on at 2.30 that afternoon when there was another 15 minute escape from the purgatory of dictation and learning John Masefield's 'Cargoes' by heart. The boy's refuge on that day over 45 years ago was in one of the windows in the kitchen block at Dudley Castle. The kitchen itself was a very high room so that the immense heat from the great fireplaces could be allowed to rise above those servants slaving away as they prepared meals for their lords and masters. A staircase led from the kitchen via a serving hatch through to the first floor where the gentry could be waited upon.

Above: What is better for improving the mind than a browse through a good book? Yet, if statistics are to be believed, our youngsters do not share those sentiments, preferring to while away their hours with Lara Croft or Game Boy on some flickering monitor in the seclusion of their bedrooms. These children were part of a generation who had to contend with the encroaching attractions of television, the goggle box in the corner of the room that stunted conversation and caused books to be left on the shelf. They were sifting though a display in the Central Library. There they could find relatively modern tales such as 'Stig of the Dump' or 'The Borrowers' to go with such classic stories as RL Stevenson's 'Treasure Island' and Daniel Defoe's 'Robinson Crusoe'. Tintin had obviously caught the imagination of the boys in the photograph, whilst the girls adopted a more historical approach in their choice of reading material. Political correctness had not been heard of in 1961 and it was perfectly normal for boys to plough through Biggles' adventures and their sisters to enjoy Enid Blyton and her

Top: There was a time when we had such powerful and impressive names for British cinemas. Palladium, Majestic, Empress and Grand had such a marvellous ring to them, certainly when compared with Screen One or Multiplex Two. The Criterion on Market Place was just one such example that Dudley could boast, a picture house that owed its existence to Woods' Vault, a 19th century drinking establishment. It was a popular meeting place for workmen and evolved into a music hall before becoming the Criterion Electric Theatre on 27 February 1911 when 'Jerusalem and the Mount of Olives' was the attraction chosen to pack 253 bottoms onto seats. For a while the back of the building was still used as a bar, but it became a dedicated cinema when this new building opened on 17 November 1923 showing 'Hearts Aflame'. The Criterion boasted a marvellous American soda fountain that made the ambience rather exciting. As the dreaded bingo made its presence felt in the 1950s audience numbers fell away and the cinema closed on 29 September 1956. Earlier in the year courting couples had sat through a double feature, 'The Extra Day' and 'Thunderstorm'. The first film featured British stalwarts Sid James, George Baker, Beryl Reid and the singer Dennis Lotis, though the starring roles went to Richard Basehart and Simone Simon. Some three hours of movies, plus a newsreel and cartoons, were completed by a love story about a Spanish fisherman falling for a mysterious girl. Only true film buffs will remember Linda Christian, Carlos Thompson and Charles Korvin from this low budget affair. The building was demolished in 1980 and replaced by a furniture store.

'Famous Five'. The library opened on St James's Road in 1909 when the senior librarians included the three daughters of William Southall who had been in charge of the former library building. Central Library had a separate reading room for ladies and, until 1933, borrowers were not allowed open access to the shelves, having to order their reading material at the counter. Dudley's local history material is now housed in a separate building at a former school in Coseley where orders have to be placed at the counter to access material.

Below: John Osborne was one of a breed of new playwrights who took the 1950s by storm with their gritty, kitchen sink drama that led to these authors being labelled 'angry young men'. Perhaps this group of drinkers at The Vine, Wolverhampton Street, linked themselves with that vogue of production because this was a pub that was once the base for Dudley Garrick Club. How differently young men dressed when out for a pint in 1956. Not for them the casual attire of jeans and T-shirt, but collar, tie and cravat. On another day the pipe smoker might even have had a neatly ironed handkerchief adorning the top pocket of his jacket. The briar clamped firmly between his teeth gave him a sophisticated, earnest look and one that oozed class and a knowledge of the way of the world. That was just what he had intended the day he had his first puff of Three Nuns and the dottle in the bottom of the bowl fizzed and spluttered as the tobacco burned down. The Vine ceased to be a recognisable pub in the 1970s, becoming a disco and wine bar as well as playing host to an Indian restaurant in the 1980s. By then these men had all reached for slippers to accompany their pipes.

Right: Ankle socks, sandal and sensible flat shoes were the fashion footwear for these young girls, though at that time they had little interest in the mid 1950s equivalent of designer gear. The boy cared more for protecting his flapping trouser legs from becoming entangled in a bicycle chain than he did for his appearance. Children were allowed to be just that and were not targeted as mini adults by fashion houses and television adverts. They had better things to do than worry about having streaks in their hair or flashing lights on their feet. Entertainment was different too, for much of it was provided by the children themselves or by making use of the simplest of equipment. A modest pair of roller skates gave them hours of fun and there were trees to be climbed and hide and seek to be played. Girls played two ball against a wall or threw jacks into the air and caught them on the backs of their hands. Yo-yos were unwound and made to arc marvellous loops with just a flick of the wrist. Boys baked conkers in the oven before taking on all comers and became adept in the art of squirting marbles into a circle scratched in the dust. Tops were whipped, hoops were bowled and no one cared a fig if you got your knees dirty.

On the home front

Below: By May 1939 even the ostrich like government had accepted what Churchill and others had been forecasting for years. War was inevitable and the little bit of paper that Neville Chamberlain waved in late 1938, proclaiming that it represented peace for our time, had been seen as an illusion. Better late than never preparations were made for the defence of our shores. There were justified fears that this war would be the one to bring civilians into the firing line. We had seen what could happen from experience of the Spanish Civil War when air raids wiped out such historic towns as Guernica, flattening buildings and killing citizens. Britain was fearful of invasion and, after the experiences of trench warfare in the 1914-18 war, of gas attack. Outside Hanson's on High Street this exercise was just one of many mounted as both a civil defence practice and lesson for the general public. Classes were given in the use of gas masks and there were even specially designed ones issued for infants. Air raid shelters were erected and evacuation procedures trialled, largely under the guidance of the Territorial Army and volunteers who had signed up for such organisations as Air Raid Precautions. When conscription was introduced on 1 May 1939 even the most ardent optimist knew that the country was heading for torrid times.

Some members of the Royal Family have the common touch, that ability to set nervous mortals at their ease when in the presence of nobility. The Duke of Kent was such a man, as can be seen on 19 February 1941 when he chatted to young civil defence cadets in Market Place during one of several visits that he made to Dudley. These teenagers, though not referred to as such for the word was not to become commonplace until the 1950s, were among the first volunteers to join a new branch of the service. Alderman AL Hillman had the bright idea of getting young people officially involved in the war effort on the home front and other towns soon adopted the measure. George, Duke of Kent seems to have had an eye for a pretty girl, but who could blame any red blooded male for enjoying a few minutes' conversation with such an attractive duo. He was the youngest surviving child of King George V and Queen Mary. Married to Princess Marina of Greece, the Duke of Kent had three children, Edward, Alexandra and Michael. He decided to do his bit for the country during the war as a member of the RAF, but sadly failed to survive the hostilities. On 24 August 1942 he was killed when a flying boat crashed during a trip to Iceland, just seven weeks after the birth of his youngest child. The 39 year old duke was the first Royal to die on active service, though Buckingham Palace said that his death was the result of an accident and not enemy action.

Eyes right by the 346 Dudley ATC Squadron was performed during a Midland Command get together at RAF Cosford in 1943-44. The squadron was formed on 21 January 1941, though the service of dedication in St Thomas's Church did not take place until 14 February 1943. Flt Lt Bob Kennedy, with his eventual successor Flt Lt Matthews at the rear, led the salute. These trainee airmen were mainly teenagers who underwent a rigorous programme of instruction before full enlistment in the RAF. It is a sobering thought to ponder on the ages of the young men in whom we entrusted the security of our skies and a

tremendous testament to their skill and bravery that they performed so heroically and successfully. Would you really trust the modern 18 year olds with the defence of the realm, once you had knocked the hamburgers from their hands or the lager cans from their mouths? Or would it be a case of if needs must and that today's youth would respond just as nobly as their grandfathers did 60 years ago? Opinions sway between the cynic and the optimist, though, if truth be known, there were probably similarly conflicting views being held when we faced the threat from the Axis powers. Let us content ourselves by recognising that these lads did us proud.

Above: Those middle years of the 20th century were nervous, anxious days as we came out of one world war and straight into further crises in the so-called peacetime. There was bloodshed in Palestine and the Berlin airlift of the late 1940s, followed by war in Korea and terrorism in Kenya in the early 1950s. The first hydrogen bomb was tested in 1952 and the spectre of communism hung over the world, causing Winston Churchill to speak of an 'iron curtain' being pulled across Europe. Fears about a nuclear holocaust and a third world war were very real, leading civil defence groups to continue the work they had performed in the 1940s and devise strategies for self protection should the worst ever come. To our jaundiced 21st century eye this exercise in operating a field kitchen looks slightly ridiculous and futile, but on 15 July 1953 it seemed to be a worthwhile activity that could save lives and provide comfort in times of need. PHG Grimmett, the emergency meals officer for Wednesbury UDC, drew off hot water from the improvised 'lazy man's boiler' as Mrs M Jacobs of the Women's Voluntary Service topped it up with fresh supplies. There was a 10 gallon oil drum inside the contraption and a pipe took the cold water to its lowest level where it could be heated and hot water then drawn off from near the top. JC Roper and Mrs M Pointon, clerk and chairman of Coseley Council respectively, were the keen observers.

The civil defence exercise was carried out at Cannon (Holdings) Ltd, Coseley, as an emergency feeding training manoeuvre organised by Staffordshire County Council for the ministry of Food. Improvised emergency cookers were built from bricks, tin and assorted rubble found on waste ground and supplemented by transportable kitchen equipment that included Bluff cookers, Triplex field cookers and Soyer boilers. Many of these had been put to good use during World War II, especially in bomb hit areas when casualties, the homeless and firefighters needed the support of food stations that could be quickly assembled. Cynics laughed at the Girl Guide nature of these field kitchens, but they had the smirks removed from their faces when they saw them in operation for real. This very equipment had done good service the previous August when floods devastated the east coast and hit a large part of Devon, washing away 36 people in Lynmouth when rivers burst their banks and swept down from the surrounding hills. People suffering the effects of disasters thanked their lucky stars for the skill and dedication of the Red Cross, WVS, St John Ambulance and similar organisations and the relief their equipment helped to bring. The appalling scene at the Aberfan school in 1966 when a coal slagheap slipped and killed 144 people, mainly children, is just one more instance of an occasion when such help was needed.

Right: Home, sweet home for this little tot was a terraced house on Himley Street. Living conditions may not have been the most luxurious, but she looked happy enough waiting for some friends to come out to play. As a little one some 40 or more years ago she did not need the trappings of modern childhood with its electronic gizmos and fancy toys. A skipping rope, an old ball, a rag doll and plenty of imagination kept the girl and her pals happy for hours on end as they played safely together in the street. Neighbours kept an eye on each other's children and grandparents often lived in the vicinity to lend a hand if they were needed. Cars roaring around the block were a danger for a future generation and the odd one that came down Himley Street moved at a sedate pace. After the war there was a great move to improve council housing stocks and large tracts of land were earmarked for development so that new estates could be built. One such project involved a 250 acre site, bought in 1947, that became the Russells Hall estate, though building work did not begin for another 10 years because of problems with ground resettlement. Houses were eventually built on concrete rafts and the work continued well into the 1960s.

Below: The family at 25 Campbell Street seems to have let all the good luck fall out of the horseshoe above its back door, but the lad in the tin bath does not look as if he is perturbed about such superstitions. For him it is an opportunity to let his imagination loose as he pilots his vessel across the seven seas doing battle with pirates or imagines that he is at the wheel of some Bugatti that once sped its way round the Brooklands circuit at a heady 75 mph. But while he was away in dreamland mum was aware of the stark realities of life on the breadline. She had a house to run and a family to feed on the shoestring that her husband's wages provided when he was lucky enough to be in work. It was a juggling exercise, moving the housekeeping money from one jar to another as she decided whether it was the rent man or the coal bill that could be paid this week. She did not have the luxuries of washing machines and tumble dryers to help her out and Monday's washday was a long grind of soaking, wringing and hanging out. The toilet was out in the back yard and you spent a penny in there with one foot firmly on the door and a loud whistle on your lips. Bath time took place in the living room in front of the fire and she cuddled up to her husband for warmth not passion at bedtime.

As part of the town's facelift after the war these houses opposite the market were demolished in 1956. The photograph is more interesting for the insight it gives into human nature, particularly that of the male. What is it about little lads that makes them want to grub about in the dust and the dirt looking for treasures with which they can fill their pockets and annoy their mums come washing day? Whilst one lad is engrossed in the ground another pesters the workmen with questions or offers of help. A third has obviously decided that he will become a traditional builder or road mender when he leaves school. Why else would he have his hands in his pockets and be generally mooching about doing not very much at all? All that he is short of is a shovel to lean on, but the workman behind him probably had plenty to spare as he enjoyed a natter with the lads as an excuse for standing around with his arms akimbo. In the 21st century he would be in danger of being accused of being a pervert, but half a century ago it was perfectly acceptable to talk to children without anyone thinking the worst. We have lost a lot of things in the name of progress and innocence is one of them.

Shopping spree

The elevated view across Market Place, taken in 1963, takes away along High Street towards St Thomas's Church, known to everyone in the town as the 'top church'. That description has nothing to do with its religious importance, being just an indication of its location. It stands in the lane once occupied by an old medieval church, but this was considered too small for the needs of an expanding parish and it was demolished in 1815. Its replacement held its first services three years later. Cars were allowed access to all of the market area in the swinging 60s, but as their numbers increased when ownership became a family necessity rather than a luxury congestion around the town centre became a major headache. Pedestrianisation of certain areas and parking and entry restrictions helped change the pattern of movement in and around Market Place, though its face remained largely unchanged. That was more than could be said for the way that Britain, as a nation, was looking. We knew that our place on the world stage had diminished since the war, but we now struggled to make our mark even in Europe. The French President, de Gaulle, rebuffed our attempts to join the Common Market with a resounding 'Non'. Things were little better at home as scandal and controversy went hand in hand. The government was rocked by the Profumo affair when it was discovered that the Minister for War had been having a relationship with a call girl, Dr Beeching wielded his axe on our railways and robbers stole over £1 million from a mail train.

Left: Looking across Market Place the far horizon is dominated by the church of St Edmund King and Martyr, or bottom church in local parlance, that is situated at the end of Castle Street. St Edmund's served the castle in medieval times and was then demolished in 1646 during the Civil War of 1642-51. When it was rebuilt in 1724 the church was a mere adjunct to St Thomas's but it regained its own individual parish status in 1844. Today the reader would be looking at this view across the top of the statue to Duncan Edwards belatedly erected in memory of Dudley's greatest sportsman, but in 1969, 11 years after his death, there would still be a long wait for a fitting memorial. Instead, you will have to be content with Lord Dudley's fountain, an edifice that is now beginning to show the ravages of time, though it maintains its importance as a piece of architectural Victoriana of cultural and nostalgic significance. As the swinging 60s drew to a close we celebrated that summer with a winner at Wimbledon in the form of Ann Jones, the Prince of Wales' investiture at Caernarvon and rock fans flocking to a festival on the Isle of Wight. Activity in Market Place would change in the following decade as a trial pedestrian only scheme was introduced on Saturdays in 1973, culminating in full closure to traffic in the 80s.

Above: The fountain on Market Place has long been a popular rendezvous for friends and sweethearts as it is such a well known and obvious landmark in Dudley. The Earl of Dudley presented it to the town in 1867 and the Countess performed the opening ceremony in front of a large and enthusiastic crowd. Some of the onlookers, whilst admiring the work of London sculptor J Forsyth, were less impressed that the fountain was intended to be, in part, a monument to the temperance movement. Albert Wood, president of the Temperance Society, gave a vote of thanks to the Earl, but others toasted their benefactor in the Coach and Horses with something a little stronger. The tree was a present from Fort William to help Dudley celebrate a 1950 Christmas. It was still a period of rationing for some goods, so the dinner plates and pudding bowls were not laden with quite as much rich fare as we now expect. But that did not stop us from enjoying the celebrations and taking great pleasure from the wide eyed youngsters' reactions when they opened their stockings. A piece of fruit at the top and a few nuts at the bottom sandwiched a toy car, a little doll, a magic colouring book and a skipping rope. They would keep the children happy for hours until dinner time when they would compete to find which one was lucky enough to bite into the silver joey, a threepenny piece inside the Christmas pud.

Below: The difference between the sexes is never more marked than when a sale is on. Men can ignore them completely, but for a woman it is that great opportunity to grab a bargain. It was more special in 1956 than it is today because we have become used to an almost permanent sale culture operated by some firms, especially the furniture stores. Their promotions are always ending next Sunday, but seem to be followed with an identical slogan as soon as Monday dawns. But for this housewife, firmly cushioned against the wilds of winter, now was one of the two main sales seasons. January had arrived and there were savings to be made. 'K' shoes had some discontinued lines at bargain prices and that should have been more than enough to entice her to open the clasp on her purse. Quite why the lines had been discontinued was kept under wraps, as was the number of these wonderful items that were for sale, but she was not to be deterred. She would be able to spot the second rate goods that had been bought in specially for this occasion, but then so could every other housewife, or so they thought. Not that it mattered, for this was a ritual to be undertaken at the start of every year and it was a long time until the summer and its round of sales. Hopefully by then the man would have finished his book.

Hall Street was about to be subjected to almost complete redevelopment in 1965. Looking down upon it from the roof of Cantor's store you can well see why. Many of the buildings were in need of money spending on them or, in some instances, being pulled down as they had outlived their usefulness. This part of town had always seemed to limp along behind the rest to some degree. Street lighting had only just been introduced when World War II broke out and, even then, suggestions were being made that Hall Street needed a face lift. When peace was declared the subject was raised again, but it took another 20 years before anything happened. The council had agreed plans in 1959 to redevelop parts of Dudley, but not a single brick was touched until the winter of 1962 and poor old Hall Street was left alone for a further three years. At long last modernisation got under way and up to date shops appeared behind wider pavements that gave pedestrians a greater degree of security and comfort than that they previously had. It is a sad irony that Hall Street today looks as bad as it ever did because parts of it were bulldozed to make way for the Southern Bypass down below its carriageway.

In 1969 Wolverhampton Street looked like a patchwork quilt as a succession of utility companies had poked about beneath its surface. As usual there was a sign warning of roadworks featuring a man digging away as hard as he could without a real one in sight. Shoppers diligently followed the arrows and crossed to the opposite pavement over the few remaining cobblestones that acted as a guide for those painters of annoying yellow lines. The young women on the right wore their skirts fashionably short, but voyeurs had to be quick to enjoy the sight of all that flesh. The maxi dress was about to be launched, much to the disgust of the majority of the male population. Their frustration would be shortlived as the next craze to hit the shops was something called hot pants, referring to the style of clothing as well as to the masculine reaction to them. Barrett's clock was showing that it was just turned noon so it would have been time to pop into the café on the right, though it referred to itself as a café, one of the quaintest examples of the use of the apostrophe even to those of us familiar with signs for teas' or potatoe's that defy the best efforts by teachers of English. A liquid lunch could be obtained at the Castle and Falcon, a Mitchell and Butler pub that was a meeting place for organisations such as Dudley Angling Society, political parties and the town soccer and cricket clubs. It closed in the 1970s and became a building society office.

Above: Wolverhampton Street is quite a narrow thoroughfare and, as this 1959 photograph demonstrates, there was only just room for two vehicles to fit side by side without encroaching onto the pavement. Its confines were recognised in the middle of the 19th century when, on 10 June 1849, it was decreed that the cattle market on Fair Days be confined to the north side of the street, both sides of Priory street and Horse Pool Green (now Stone Street). Cattle were not to stand on the south side of Wolverhampton Street. The whole idea of herds of animals milling around in such a confined space is difficult to take on board, though if anyone has ever been to the summer sales at a major retail outlet he might have some notion of what was involved. Locals out window shopping for shoes or rainwear were witnessing the last years of the traditional mode of shopping in outlets that had changed little in style since before the war. The swinging 60s would introduce boutiques and unisex to the High Streets of Britain and piped pop music would accompany every purchase. As the 70s came in smaller, family stores were swallowed up by the big chains and the opportunities to stand on a pavement and gaze inside the display window became ever more rare.

Left: In the mid 1950s men could not be trusted to do the shopping properly, so they had to be given a list on which the wife had written clear instructions. This was then handed to the shop assistant who treated her customer with as much disdain as it was possible to get away with. Behind her head was an array of medicines, potions, perfumes and waters that would only have confused the poor chap. The contents of the Goya display on the counter would have flummoxed him completely. To let him come in and make a choice or even be left to his own devices was a recipe for disaster. On the occasion when he wanted a nice birthday present for the missus the assistant made the selection on his behalf. Looking at this photograph must conjure up vivid memories for readers born in the baby boom postwar years. This is how the shops were when they were children, shelves piled high with bottles, tins and packets and not a security camera in sight. Goods were scattered on the counter and you could see what it was you were purchasing as the items were not completely enveloped in plastic and packaging. However, this customer was not concerned about the surroundings because he just wanted to get out of the shop before any of his pals saw him doing women's work.

Above: The short back and sides, with a dab of Brylcreeem to keep hair in place, was the simple requirement of nearly all men in 1955. A barber's job was a relatively easy task. Before long Teddy Boys were expecting large quiffs at the front, square necks at the back and carefully shaped sideburns by their ears. The poor old man under the striped pole had worse to contend with in the next couple of decades as Beatle hairdos, Brian Jones mops, highlights and curly perms all made their mark. The man concentrating on the racing form in his paper on a Saturday afternoon in Market Place was picking out a winner, but would have no betting shop where he could have a flutter. Such an establishment was an invention of the 1960s and his money had to be slipped to a runner or handed over quietly in the back room of a pub. If he let his eyes wander from the list of runners and riders he might have spotted the advert for one of the films showing in town that week. 'The End of the Affair', based on the successful novel by Graham Greene, starred Deborah Kerr and Van Johnson, with support from John Mills and Peter Cushing. Despite such a star studded cast it was not a box office hit, possibly because it dealt with a gloomy affair in wartime London, religious guilt and death. In the mid 50s cinema audiences wanted escapism, not miserable reminders of times they wanted to put behind them. A 1999 remake with Ralph Fiennes and Julianne Moore was much more successful.

Some parts of Dudley have changed little since the war and, even if the names on shops have altered and some buildings disappeared, the view is still essentially the same. That cannot be said for Hall Street for who would now guess that the camera was pointed towards Market Place where Tyler's and Dudley's oldest shoe shop once stood? Traffic lights and the King Street roundabout with Trindle Road now dominate the end of Hall Street with a view across to the Churchill Precinct that offers a different style of shopping than was on offer in 1957. Clydesdale was having a Spring Sale and further along the east side of the street there seemed to be some interest in what was on offer in Broadmead's. In between these shops Kendall's butcher's seemed to be getting ready to call it a day as the longer evening shadows began to stretch across the roadway. The usual supply of gamebirds hanging on hooks in the window had been taken down and the trays of homemade sausages put away for another day. The butcher always regarded himself as the housewife's friend and could be relied upon to have a special cut prepared for his favourite customer. Little did she know that the minute she left the shop another favourite would walk in through the door.

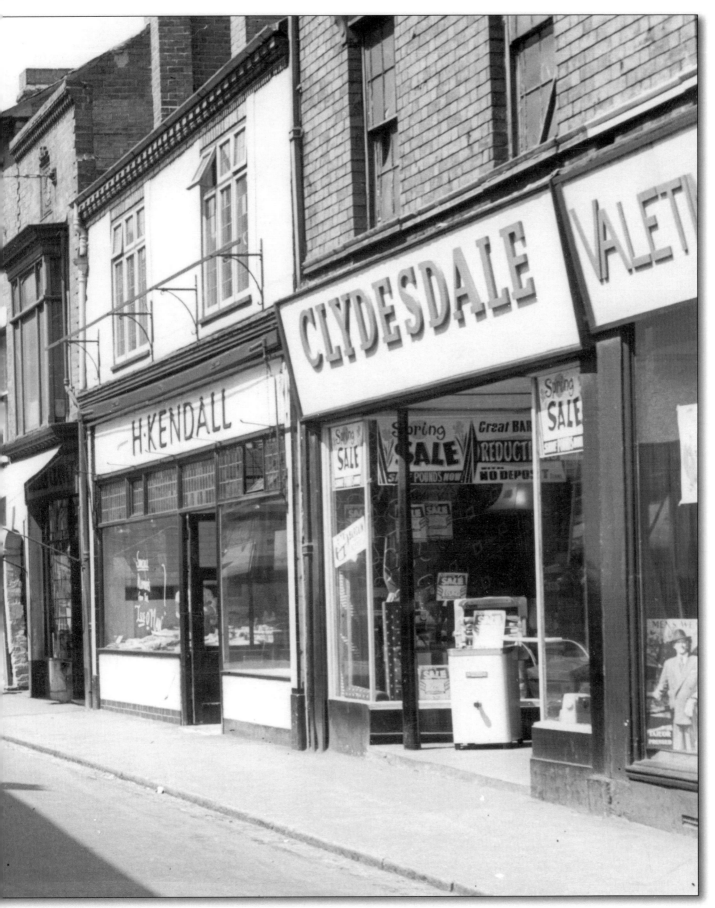

On the move

Below: Looking along Stafford Street from Wellington Road in 1955 perhaps the knot of people on the pavement was discussing the news that femme fatale and murderer Ruth Ellis was about to go into the record books as the last woman to be hanged in this country, though no one realised the significance of the case at the time. If they had more cheery things to discuss these locals could have commented on the success of Donald Campbell on Ullswater where he and his Bluebird had pushed the world waterspeed record to 202 mph. Across the big pond Walt Disney had opened Disneyland in California, but it was something out of the reach of most British tourists who had to be content with holidays in Llandudno or Colwyn Bay. The discussion group was photographed from a spot roughly opposite where the modern leisure centre now stands, with Oxford Street leading away to the right under the advert for Cherry Blossom shoe polish. It is less than 50 years ago, but the horse and cart was still a familiar sight on our streets. That acts as a reminder to today's population of how the pace of life has quickened in the intervening years. We ambled around the streets and took time out for a chat, rather than rushing hither and thither without a moment to spare.

An autoclave is a piece of equipment used for establishing and maintaining high temperatures needed in a variety of manufacturing processes, whilst being capable of withstanding strong pressure. This monster, that had come to rest on High Street in 1962, measured 64 feet in length and had a circumference of 20 feet. Weighing in at 22 tons it was bound for the Northern Brick Company, County Antrim to be used in the production of lime/sand autoclave bricks. Dudley had a number of its own brickworks, including the well known Stourbridge Glazed Brick and Fire Clay Company at Blowers Green. The town had seen other large pieces of engineering pass by over the years thanks to its being one of the early centres of the industrial revolution. Deposits of coal, iron ore, limestone and fireclay gave it an enviable position in the district's economy and Dudley is particularly proud of its contribution to the wealth of the Black Country. Perhaps one of the most memorable pieces of equipment ever turned out came from the Chain and Anchor Works, owned by Noah Hingley and Sons. The plant was built at Netherton in 1845 and the company provided the huge 16 ton anchor for the ill fated 'Titanic' that foundered in the Atlantic icefield in 1912.

This dramatic night-time view of the market, looking towards the top church, St Thomas's, was taken in the mid 1960s. The market stalls had all been bedded down for the night and the lights shone in a dazzling fashion from the shop windows, advertising signs and street lamps. The market has been with us for nearly 750 years, but has always kept its importance as a focal point for Dudley shoppers. There have been some major changes since this photograph was taken as the old cobblestones have disappeared and Market Place made into a pedestrianised zone. Towards the end of the last century the market was reroofed and now has 74 stalls selling a mixed bag of goods six days a week. Market Place itself only came into being in the 1840s, formerly being the site where the old town hall stood. Traffic used to pass around the stalls in a clockwise direction before vehicles were banned in the early 1980s. Over to the right the names on the buildings included Zissman's, Bell's, Hearnshaw's carpets, British Home Stores and the Midland Bank. Some of them have flourished in the intervening years, while others have gone to that great retailer in the sky.

Above: Moving house or getting married are supposed to be up near the top of the list for stressful situations, but at least they only occur occasionally in anyone's life. Sitting in a traffic jam surely knocks these into a cocked hat because it is an almost daily occurrence that seems to be insoluble. As we fret and fume behind the wheel, tempers fraying and more smoke coming out of our ears than through any leaky exhaust, spare a moment to reflect on how it used to be. We had the open road, traffic bowling along merrily and AA patrolmen with all the time in the world to give a member a respectful salute with his gauntleted hand as he rode by on his motorbike and sidecar. Think again and look at this scene outside the Midland Red bus station on Birmingham Road on 3 July 1951 that includes a motor cyclist who looks suspiciously like an early version of Benny Hill's Fred Scuttle in his distinctive beret. Over half a century ago, even with far less car ownership, the evening rush hour was a horrendous experience for those trapped outside the depot at 5.40 pm. The bus station opened on 2 August 1929, but it was a cramped design and manoeuvrability inside was difficult, especially when newer, bigger buses were added to the service. Congestion became more and more problematic, but the depot was not demolished until 1994 when it made way for the new A461 Southern Bypass.

Above right: An extensive continental food market now stands near the corner of Edward Street in this now run down part of town from where this view of Stafford Street was taken in 1959, looking across Wellington Road and Southall Lane. There are still some outlets of interest to the motorist in this vicinity, as there were over 40 years ago when the Fina garage, car showroom and Eccles re-tyring service traded here. The lonely, abandoned cart on the right may have belonged to a window cleaner, but he must have been operating at ground floor level or getting a refill for his bucket as his ladders have been left behind. As the 1950s drew to a close cars began to develop more aggressive styling. The radiator grilles took on the appearance of large grimacing faces and huge bumpers threatened to sweep pedestrians and cyclists aside as chrome became king. As the next decade took shape so did the wings on automobiles. Distinctive fins became a feature on such as the Vauxhall Victor, but their attraction was shortlived. They proved to be rust traps and pound notes were of more importance to the average motorist than some vaguely transatlantic styling. Some car owners had to acquire skills in the use of fibreglass as they patched up the holes.

Far right: In 1958 a learner driver was heading along Wolverhampton Street away from the Regent petrol station towards the junction with Charlton Street. If the driver intended to turn left at that point it would have been a good opportunity to practice hand signals. There was a part of the driving test that demanded that a driver demonstrated his knowledge of their use because not every vehicle on the road was fitted with winking indicators. Some older cars had no

means of indicating and even with modern models many still had semaphore arms that popped up from the side of the car when a lever on the driving wheel was moved across. They were difficult to spot and were more likely to poke out an eye of an unwary cyclist than afford any clear notice of intent to turn right or left. Younger motorists will be amused to be told that poking an arm out of the car window and rotating it in a circular motion meant that the driver was not suffering from some form of insanity but was merely trying to show other road users that he was about to turn left. Tell them that pretending to bounce a basketball outside the driver's door showed that the car was about to slow down and you will be institution-alised immediately.

lobal warming, the melting of ice caps and the greenhouse effect have all been blamed for the warmer winters and wetter winters that we seem to have been experiencing in recent years. If that is the case then what was going on in 1951? Stafford Street was awash as the heaviest day's rainfall in an already wet month had been deposited on the town. The roof mounted wipers on the car were having little effect as the driver attempted to make some progress and we can only hope that his sunroof did not spring a leak. People blamed those testing the atom bomb for disturbing weather patterns as this was August and they should have been enjoying balmy summer days instead of scurrying for cover. Others blamed the Russians and decided that it was some sort of Communist plot to bring havoc to our shores, probably as the result of secret information that Burgess and MacLean had taken with them when the former diplomats disappeared from Washington and made their way to Moscow. 'Reds under the beds' was a popular fear and one held particularly dear by Senator Joseph McCarthy who instituted witch hunts within the State Department and movie industry in a later discredited attempt to rid America of left wing sympathisers.

Below centre: The volume of traffic has changed dramatically since 1958 when this junction of Furnace Road, Churchfield Street and King Street, looking west towards High Side on High Street, was photographed. The road from Halesowen and Stourbridge, to the left, is now full of cars at any time of the day heading towards the town centre or working their way around towards the back of the Churchill Precinct and the Southern Bypass roundabout at the bottom of Castle Hill. The two wheeler heading towards the camera is a period piece, as is the duffel coat the rider is wearing. It was a style of topcoat beloved of students and earnest young men who met to discuss politics, literature and the iniquities of nuclear warfare. This rider was one of the early wave who rejected motorbikes in favour of scooters and spawned the beginnings of a rivalry that continued through the 1960s. Greasy haired, leather jacketed rockers on bikes, meeting at cafés where Gene Vincent music blared out, were the arch enemies of long haired, long coated mods who preferred to listen to the Small Faces. The antagonism between the two factions came to a head at Bank Holidays when seaside resorts were turned into battlegrounds. On occasions police would mount roadblocks and turn both groups back on the outskirts of town.

Bottom: In 1960 cars and buses used our roads in harmony with one another. Pictured by the terminus in Stone Street there was no sense of the pressure that the car owner would come to feel in subsequent years as dedicated bus lanes, one way systems, restricted zones and swingeing parking charges all conspired to make him feel unwanted. Horse drawn trams, later supported by steam power that was introduced in the 1880s, provided the first large scale public transport in Dudley. Lines were electrified in 1899 and the clanking trams that would later inspire Judy Garland to burst her lungs on 'The Trolley Song' in the 1944 film 'Meet me in St Louis' dominated Dudley's streets until after World War One. Between the wars trams had to share their routes with the trolley buses that first took to the streets in 1923. Pedestrians were wary of the new mode of public transport because they could hear the noisy trams making their way along the road behind them, but the trolley buses were a quieter breed and were involved in a number of unfortunate accidents that had them unkindly dubbed 'the whispering death'. As petrol engined buses also began to make their mark the days of trams were numbered and they failed to survive beyond the end of the 1930s. Trolley buses continued to swing their arms into the air until 5 March 1967 when the last one made the journey from Wolverhampton.

Making a living

Below: Rag and bone men were not usually as smartly groomed as this chap on Hill Street, Netherton c1956, so it is probably safe to say that he had been forewarned that a photographer was in the area. Perched on the back of his cart, in amongst the scrap metal, wheels and axles that some child might have been glad of to make the chassis for a soapbox car, was a cardboard box containing donkey stones for the housewives. They brought him their superfluous bits and pieces and he provided them with the wherewithal to make the front step a smart threshold that no mother in law could ever criticise. To see a woman in a flowery pinny on her hands and knees scrubbing away at the little block of stone by the front door was a common sight as each tried to outdo her neighbour. When dad came home he was careful to stride across the gleaming surface or face the wrath of the one who really wore the trousers. Children loved to listen out for the cry of 'rag-bone' echoing across the cobbles, for they could run out into the street and hitch a lift for a couple of blocks until they were booted off. Grandad was equally pleased to hear the sound because he could get his bucket and shovel and scrape up the necessary for his rhubarb down on the allotment.

The number of scouts required to change a light bulb is not documented, but it took nine of them to attend to car cleaning duties at Dudley Grammar School in 1951. Maybe it was one of the masters' cars that was getting a good going over, so making sure that the next time one of these lads was unable to conjugate his Latin verbs the swish of the cane would be excused for once. It was Bob-a-job Week and the troop of youngsters put their backs into the task, though their reward would only work out at just over a penny per head if the customer adhered to the going rate. Whatever he stumped up would be accepted with thanks because children did not question their teachers or even regard them as fellow human beings. They lived in a room marked 'Staff' that was forever clouded in tobacco smoke and contained piles of exercise books and bottles of red ink. Teachers went in there at four o'clock every evening and reappeared, long gowns billowing out behind them, to walk the corridors the following morning on their way to the assembly hall in time for morning prayers and the usual lecture about the toilets from the headmaster. They did not have Christian names nor anything normal like a wife and children of their own, or so it appeared to their pupils. Perhaps teachers were born as fully grown adults because you could never imagine that they had played conkers or climbed trees and once been normal lads.

The rubble and shattered brickwork in the foreground might make you think that this is the result of some wartime bombing raid, but on closer inspection of the shops and cars it becomes obvious that this is a scene from the end of the 1960s. Despite being a listed building, the Dudley Arms Hotel at 39 High Street, Market Place was being pulled down to make way for an extension to Marks and Spencer. It was another example of heritage giving way to so called progress that blighted the face of so many English towns at the time. There had been a pub on this site since the reign of Queen Anne. Originally the Rose and Crown, it was rebuilt in 1786 and given the name that would serve it well for nearly two centuries. The site had been the subject of a 1,000 year lease from Lord Dudley at a nominal rent. In its heyday the Dudley Arms boasted bars, sitting rooms and kitchens on the ground floor, with four bedrooms and a resplendent billiard room above and 12 more bedrooms on the second floor. The livery stables had room for 32 horses and carriage places, plus the hotel's very own blacksmith's shop and harness rooms. The only remnants of this fine hostelry that have survived can be found in the Black Country Museum and the Talbot Hotel, Stourbridge. The former has the old coat of arms and the latter has one of the fine stained glass windows.

Above: Think of school dinners and memories come flooding back of tough boiled spuds with little black bits in them, stringy meat that you would not have given the cat and vegetables that required the kiss of life after spending all morning drowning in some huge pan. Semolina with a blob of jam in the middle was something to look forward to after the delights of the main course, with sago as an alternative every third day. How ironic it was that we had to say grace and thank the good Lord for providing the stuff on our plates that we were only interested in disposing of as quickly as possible so that we could get our game of playground football under way again. Some children got free school meals and, although the teachers tried to disguise who they were, everyone knew their identity because why else did they remain in their seats on Monday morning as the rest of us queued with our five shillings? Posher schools expected the money to be paid up front for a whole term in advance. School dinners have moved on since those days, or so the powers that be would have you believe. Certainly, even as long ago as 1962 the dinner ladies at Dudley Grammar School were preparing something more interesting than the usual run of the mill fare we were used to.

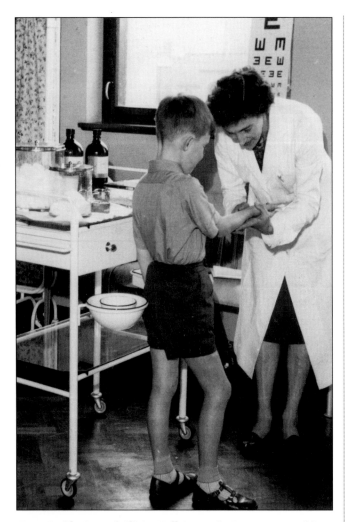

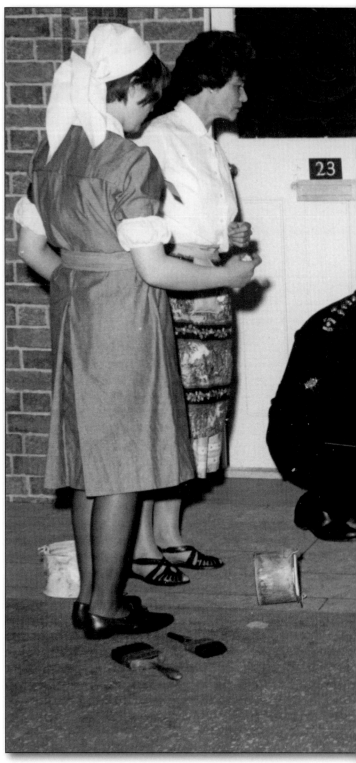

Top: Inside Central Clinic, Hall Street, in June 1962, as this lad was being checked over, it seems difficult to appreciate that the National Health Service had only been with us for less than 14 years. It was in July 1948 that the Labour government, with Health Minister Aneurin Bevan leading the way, formally introduced what was seen as the most sweeping reform of any that had been part of its manifesto that brought Attlee to power in 1945. Free medical treatment for the entire population, now taken for granted by those of us born in the years since the war, was a revolutionary idea that had not been universally popular. Not surprisingly, reactionaries in the medical profession saw their mystique disappearing and their power being eroded. A leading surgeon, John Dickson Wright, complained that doctors would become paid servants to an army of civil servants, while Lord Horder, chairman of the BMA, spoke of 'selling our heritage'. Despite these misgivings both the medical profession and the general public soon embraced the new order. Babies drank down their free orange juice, shortsighted youngsters pulled on their pink-coated specs and opened wide for the dentist to probe away. Nitty Nora, the school nurse, examined heads and dished out evil smelling shampoo so that mum could rid us of the creepy-crawlies that must have come from the scruffy kid sitting next to us in class.

Above: The pots of paint scattered around the foot of the ladder were part of the props used to make this exercise more realistic. The St John Ambulance officer was not taking down the unfortunate decorator's last will and testament, but recording observations and marks to be awarded to the angels of mercy tending to the broken bones and lacerations supposedly suffered in a fall from a dizzy height. The injuries were imaginary as this was a staged incident, but the cadets'

performance was important. They were practising the skills that would be required in a real life situation and were carrying them out under some pressure because the trainees were taking part in the nursing cadet finals, a national competition of some prestige. Teams from all over Britain had won through a variety of local and county heats to participate as one of the 12 regional finalists for the title of Top First Aiders for 1965, presented by Kenneth Robinson,

the Health Minister. Joan Woodall, Janet Thomson, Janice Upton and Joan Carrington represented St John Ambulance Brigade, Worcestershire (Dudley Nursing Cadet Division). Linda Beecheno acted as a reserve, possibly because her Christian name did not begin with a 'J' rather than in any reflection upon her abilities. Whether the house painting was ever finished is not recorded, but Dudley's nurse cadets performed their tasks admirably.

Moving Round

Goods have needed to be moved around since time immemorial. If 'Early Man' wanted to move something he slung it over his shoulder, and if it was too heavy to lift he left it where it was. Later the domestication of the first horses led to the use of packhorses whilst the later invention of the wheel and the horse collar allowed loads, far greater than anything which could be moved by manpower alone, to be shifted vast distances.

Those who owned a horse and cart soon found that they could make a living, not simply moving their own property, but those of other people for a fee, and the transport industry was born. In this country, for untold centuries, and still just within living memory, transport by horse and cart was still something which could be seen on our roads every day. Running a small haulage firm was something which anyone with a horse could easily do and many individuals did so. But relatively few of the firms which started life in the horse and cart days survive to this day. Sometimes the firms died with their owners, sometimes they were simply unable or unwilling to move with the times and trade in their horses for motor vehicles and sometimes they failed, through lack of business skills and became unviable. One local firm however which has not only survived but prospered for more than a hundred years is that of William Round (Transport) Ltd, a firm which over the decades has been prepared to tackle anything - including once shipping an elephant!

The firm was founded in 1884 by William Round helped by his wife Sara Jane. Before starting out on his own William had helped his father, also a haulage contractor, with his horses.

Above: Founder William Round and son Arthur.
Below: William Round pictured at the rear of a 1930s removal van with son Arthur (centre) and nephew Bert (right) who was with the company all his working life.

With his own horse and cart William set out delivering bricks, coal and undertaking furniture removals around Dudley.

Initially based in Cross Street the firm soon moved to Greystone Passage, Dudley where it would remain for many decades before moving to Harts Hill.

At Greystone Passage, William, Sara and their young family would have room not only for their horses but they would also keep pigs and chickens. A small sideline was to charge people to bring their sows to be serviced by the Rounds' boar.

The founder's sons, William, Bert and lastly Arthur, born in 1913, would all eventually follow their father into the haulage business, though sadly Bert was killed in the first world war. In turn Arthur's sons; Bill, John and Alan, and daughter Carole, all joined the firm.

Three generations have been involved with the business and eventually the family would occupy not only a garage but a yard and five houses in Greystone Passage.

In the early 1920s young Arthur would work with his brother Bill driving a cart pulled by Bill's horse, Boxer.

Arthur, aged just 12, would follow with his own cart drawn by another horse, Little Titch, and would go and collect the shavings from Shuttleworths in King Street twice a week; in order to collect the shavings Arthur used a trolley which could carry eight bags of shavings at a time; once, as he was pushing the trolley back to Shuttleworths down the narrow road, a vehicle reversing from Hansons Brewery caught the side of the trolley and spun it around pinning Arthur against the wall and crushing his leg; it would be a long time before Arthur could go to school again. Arthur's mother got £25 compensation for his injured leg - compensation was far more modest in those days than it has become in our day.

Eventually Arthur was well enough to return to St Thomas' School in King Street where he would stay until the age of 14 before joining his father and older brother.

By then Arthur's older brother Bill was driving a large motor van. Though many may have thought that there would always be a need for horses the investment on a motor vehicle was seen as essential to enable the firm to make long distance deliveries and such foresight would prove to be all too accurate. Of course all kinds of transport were becoming motorised during this period: one unusual contract at this time, and one of Arthur's regular jobs was to move used tickets from the Midland Red bus garage in Birmingham New Road and take them to the tip on the horse cart, he also used to collect pig iron from the station for delivery as well as moving loads of rubbish from the co-op in Charles Street.

At the age of 17 Arthur's father allowed him to take on the Ford Van which until then his brother Bill had driven; brother Bill got a new Dennis van. The business now got regular work delivering bedroom suites and furniture from shops to customers' houses. The vans used had modified bodywork which included a Davis Smith West Brom Motor Vehicle

Above: *A 1924 Registration Book for William Round's first removals vehicle, a Ford truck, pictured above left.* **Left:** *William outside the company's Greystone Passage garage.*

chassis which gave the vans longer bodies enabling them to carry more goods.

The 1930s saw the worst economic crash ever experienced in Britain; the 'Hungry Thirties' as they were known saw millions on the dole and a falling off of trade all over the world. The Midlands were not exempt from the Great Depression but somehow the small firm of William Round managed to keep going taking any job that could be found. And despite these problems and the looming threat of German rearmament hope springs eternal in the human breast and never less so when a young man finds the girl of his dreams.

Young Arthur had married Sarah Ann Dutton in 1936 when he was 23 and she 21. The future for them and the firm looked bright and the business moved to

Stourbridge Road, Hartshill where it began to develop and grow. Needless to say however nothing ever runs quite as smoothly as we would hope.

Immediately before the outbreak of the second world war the firm had four vans and some good contracts for example working for the CWS in Hall Street, Dudley, travelling every night to London. In 1939, however, all the vehicles were commandeered for the war effort. They and their drivers were attached to the Hartlebury Depot to collect goods for the war effort delivering aircraft parts day and night to London and all over the country.

Above: From left to right, Arthur Round, and sons John, Alan and Bill. Below: A William Round removals lorry built by Cartwright Coachbuilders in the 1970s.

At the end of the war the CWS delivery contract was renewed, delivering self-service fittings, which would last for forty years. At the same time Arthur formed a long lived partnership with Mr Leonard Hepburn, in charge of a company at Tipton. Wm Round were given a contract to supply two HGVs a day which increased over the years to

eight and then to twenty plus drivers on a daily basis. This partnership lasted for some fifty years providing a first class service, with some drivers spending most of their working lives on this contract.

The company also supplied two vehicles to collect the News of the World and Sunday Mirror from Dudley station for delivery to local newsagents in the Dudley area.

The firm bought land in 1981 on the site of what had once been the Pink House and the Lime Light Cinema; in the process they found all the workings of the engines which used to be played at the cinema. They donated these to the Black Country Museum to be shown to future generations.

Today main activities remain general haulage, furniture removal and distribution for the furniture trade both in the UK and overseas to Ireland and Spain.

How has this firm survived and prospered for well over a century? The answer is a simple one and encapsulated in a simple but effective philosophy handed down over the years 'always on time, always helpful'.

The company is grateful for the total support given by staff and drivers who have worked for the business for many years helping to build and maintain the fine reputation first established by the founder of this enduring family business, William Round, far back in the closing decades of the 19th century.

Today the name of removal specialists William Round (Transport) Ltd is a familiar one to Dudley residents who regularly see the William Round name emblazoned on the side of the firm's vans as they make their way around Dudley. And to those Dudley residents who travel further afield and encounter the distinctive William Round vans in far flung parts of Britain the name is not only a welcome reminder of home but also a source of pride that a small Dudley firm has not only survived in the turbulent word of commerce for well over a century but that it has prospered despite all the trials and tribulations of wars, recessions and petrol rationing: well done!

Top left: *Arthur with the family dog at Greystone Passage on land he would later have his house built.*
Top right: *Arthur and wife Sarah celebrating their Golden Wedding anniversary with family, (back row left to right) Bill, Carole, Alan and John.* ***Left:*** *Arthur, Alan, William, Carole and John Round in front of one of their large fleet of vehicles, August 2002.*

Learning for life

Today the minimum school leaving age is 16 though many readers of this book will no doubt recall entering the world of work at the age of 14. Not that being thrust out of the classroom was necessarily the end of our association with textbooks and tests. There cannot be many of us who have not had some kind of further education. For some such experiences have been vocational, learning the skills of a trade or profession; for others it has been academic, perhaps getting a few extra O levels or maybe attending courses simply for the love of learning.

These days we are a nation of astonishingly well educated people. But it wasn't always so. Few of us need delve too far back into family history to find marriage registers and other documents signed with a cross rather than a signature. In the 19th century a wave of self improvement programmes arose, supported both by both public legislation and private charity. Though some objected that teaching every child to write would simply lead to graffiti appearing lower down on walls, the needs of the emerging industrial society for both skilled and literate workers who could exploit the then new technologies such as engineering, electricity and steam made the systematised expansion of technical education imperative. And not least in towns like Dudley.

Today Dudley College is a General Further Education College serving the West Midlands but with students drawn from around both Britain and the world. It is one of the largest FE colleges in the United Kingdom and delivers a diverse range of courses to full and part-time students both on and off campus. The College's aim is to provide the highest quality education and training, an aim

Above: *The Chemical Laboratory, circa 1910.*
Below: *An aerial view of Dudley and Staffordshire Technical College, circa 1937.*

College to provide Technical Education facilities for Dudley and the surrounding areas. A site of five acres at Broadway was eventually offered by the Dudley Town Council in 1927.

Plans for a new College were drawn up and found to cost £136,000. With only £77,500 available however the Governors decided to build only part of the plan - the lower ground floor, the main ground floor (minus the planned assembly hall and gym) and a portion of the planned first floor.

Due to a number of problems building did not actually begin until May 1931 after a tender of £74,177 had been accepted. The whole project, including furniture and equipment would cost a little over £100,000, of which the Miner's Welfare Committee notably contributed £6,000.

Happily, before the project was complete, money was found to build the octagonal Assembly Hall as originally planned and which was completed in time for the first admission of students in September 1935. The following March the Dudley and Staffordshire Technical College was formally opened by Earl de la Warr, Parliamentary Secretary to the President of the Board of Education.

The outbreak of war in 1939 led to the postponement of plans to complete the College and although a recommendation was made that a new Engineering Workshop should

reflected in the College's mission statement: Serving the community through world class, high quality education and training. The College campus now includes premises in Broadway, Wolverhampton Street, Mons Hill and the Rowley Regis Centre but the origins of the College were far more modest.

Dudley College traces its origins to 1862 and to the building of the Dudley Public Hall and Mechanics Institute to provide for the technical, recreational and vocational needs of students.

About 1896 additional accommodation in Stafford Street, known as the Lancastrian Board School was acquired and became the Dudley Technical School (renamed the Dudley Technical College in 1928). These premises were however unsuitable and in 1918 agreement was reached between Dudley and Staffordshire Education Committees to erect a

Top left: *The Cookery Room in the 1930s.*
Top right: *The Gymnasium, 1930s.* **Above:** *The Foundry, circa 1936.* **Right:** *The Engineering Workshop.*

be built, even its construction was not complete until 1948.

In the meantime a Junior Technical and Commercial School had been established within the College in 1937 and accommodation was also provided for the Dudley and Maria Grey Training Colleges during the war. The College was also actively engaged in the war effort, not least in radio training for RAF personnel and the education of air crew.

In 1947 it was decided that Dudley's School of Arts and Crafts should be administrated as a Department of the Technical College and be transferred from its home in St James' Road to Broadway: astonishingly it would take 30 years for the decision to be implemented, although a similar decision to incorporate the Dudley Evening Institute bore more immediate fruit.

Departments of Mechanical, Structural and Electrical Engineering were formed in 1948 and a Department of Production Engineering - along with the now somewhat sexist-sounding Department of Women's Subjects. The following year the Engineering Workshop was extended to accommodate Metallurgy, Metrology and a Fitting Shop; (the block would be further extended in 1955 to include an Electrical Installation Workshop, Soil Mechanics and Craft Sciences Laboratories).

Since the building of the College an unusual situation had existed in which the Principals of Wednesbury Technical College and Cannock Mining Technical College had been nominally the heads of the Metallurgy and Mining Depart-

ments in Dudley. This arrangement was terminated in 1953.

In 1960 Arnold W Gibson, who astonishingly had been Principal since 1928, died and was succeeded by Sidney H Hoxey. The new Principal would see some significant changes to the College during his short period in post.

A momentous year in the life of the College arrived in 1966; that April saw the joint arrangements for the administration of the College by Staffordshire and Dudley terminated by Local Authority boundary changes. The College now became solely the responsibility of the Dudley Authority and was renamed the Dudley Technical College again after more than 30 years as the Dudley and Staffordshire Technical College. The cost to the Dudley Authority to compensate Staffordshire for its loss was less than £100,000.

That September the Department of Art was moved from St James Road to another unsatisfactory site the vacant Holly Hall Junior School. Principal SC Hoxey now died and his deputy Donald Bailey succeeded him and would lead the College for almost 20 years.

Top right: *The Welding Shop.* **Above:** *The Chemical Laboratory, circa 1910.* **Left:** *The Machine Drawing Room, circa 1912.*

Shortage of space however continued to be a problem and in 1968 the Tipton Annexe (formerly the Tipton Council Offices) was occupied by the College and used to accommodate construction and associated courses.

The 1965/66 building programme in the two areas each side of the Main Hall and to the left of the Entrance Foyer was completed early in 1968 and consisted of a Board Room, offices, classrooms and laboratories. The same programme extended the student refectory as well as providing garage and storage space underneath.

F-Block too would be completed in 1968. The block had been started many years earlier as a student project of one storey but had then been demolished to make way for the new two storey building. The same programme also included Motor Vehicle, Electrical and Hydraulic Laboratories.

Around the same time an amalgamation of the Brierley Hill School of Art with the College's Department of Art was completed and some rationalisation of Art occurred between the two adjacent annexes at Holly Hall and Brierley Hill.

Top left: *Electrical Engineering Laboratory, circa 1937.*
Above right: *The Main Entrance Hall in the 1930s.*
Below: *An aerial view of the Broadway site.*

Proposals to develop a Glass Centre at the Brierley Hill Annexe came to fruition in 1971 as well as the establishment of Heavy Vehicle courses at a new annexe at Brockmoor.

The following year a College Medical Service was provided for the first time with a full-time nurse and a doctor who appeared for two hours each week. The new Medical Service would be housed along with the Student Counsellor and the Careers Counsellor in the former Caretaker's Flat.

The new Glass Centre was formally opened in October 1973 by HRH the Duchess of Kent. The Glass Centre would continue to grow over the following years, such growth becoming possible by the transfer of the Library and Glass Museum from the Annexe to other premises as the Glass Centre grew to fill the whole of the ground floor and some of the upper floor.

In 1979 when a road widening scheme threatened the Holly Hall Annexe, Art was finally brought to the Main College (a move which had been approved as long ago as 1947). That same year, to reflect the changing

years at the College and was succeeded in January 1986 by his Vice Principal, Gordon Hopkins. In those 28 years Donald Bailey had presided over a remarkable period of growth and change for the College. The physical expansion of the College would be a reflection of the considerable expansion of academic, vocational and training courses throughout the period.

By now the College was providing a comprehensive range of vocational courses in Engineering, Electronics, Construction, Motor Vehicle Work, Business Studies, Secretarial and Hair Dressing as well as the less conventional courses in glass and drop forging technology. At the same time the College had responded to the academic and cultural needs of young and old alike with a wide range of courses for GCEs, domestic subjects and a wide range of Arts and Crafts

pattern of further Education, the name of the College was now changed to the Dudley College of Technology.

During the 1970s the College had continued to expand, especially in the fields of computing and community care. An early involvement in computing provided the opportunity for the College to later move easily into the world of microprocessing, microcomputing, robotics and other computer -aided processes. By the middle 1980s the College had become a nationally recognised centre of excellence in computer related studies leading in 1983 and 1984 respectively to the opening of both an Information Technology Centre and an Open Access Practical Training Facility.

In 1982 Dudley Language and Literacy Centre was transferred to the control of the College and the following year Adult Education in the old Borough of Dudley was returned to the College after an absence of ten years. In 1985 the Dudley Education and Training Centre was also transferred to the control of the College.

That same year would see the acquisition of the Wolverhampton Street School and the nearby Old Bakery by the College and new purpose built accommodation being built on the site.

In December 1985 Principal, Donald Bailey announced his retirement after 28

The following years would see no slowing of the growth and change which had been so characteristic of the post-war decades.

Since its establishment in 1862 Dudley College has met the needs of the local community through the provision of a

*Top left: A view of the College from the extensive grounds. **Above right:** A view of the College through the Priory Garden ruins. **Right:** 21st Century technology at work in the Classroom.*

stimulating and invigorating environment for the acquisition of knowledge and a commitment to being at the cutting edge of developments in teaching and learning The results speak for themselves with over 20,000 students achieving awards each year, in excess of 600 students move on from the College to places in Universities and other Higher education establishments, more than 800 students graduate from the College with HND or HNC qualifications and many thousands more leave the College not only with a new qualification but also with a higher self-esteem having achieved something that may have seemed impossible to them a year earlier.

The College strives to provide a first class environment for students and to achieve this has invested heavily in new technology.

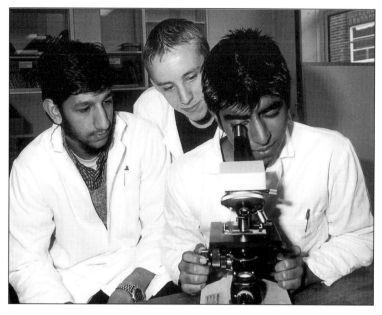

The College also provides education and training services to students who are unable or unwilling to attend the College premises. Outreach facilities include the provision of education in nine of HM's prisons, the operation of a Centre for Learning at Longbridge in association with the MG Rover Group which provides education and training for its employees and families, employees of companies in MG's supply chain and members of the local community. Also the 'Waterfront4Training' at Merry Hill provides an access point for training of all the employees of companies at Merry Hill, as well as being an access point for Learndirect and the operation of a number of outreach centres throughout the West Midlands, where those who would otherwise find it impossible to attend college can benefit from the education and training provide by the College's Outreach division and its partners.

The opportunities offered by Midlands Oak Skills and Technology Ltd (MOST), a subsidiary acquired in 2000, offers quality training in association with the local TECs and privately funded training for local companies, again expanding and extending the facilities offered to local people.

Such achievements confirm the position of Dudley College as one of the premier Further Education Colleges in the United Kingdom and at the beginning of the 21st Century, still led by Principal and Chief Executive Dr Gordon Hopkins, the future of the College looks every bit as promising as its illustrious past.

Top right: *Science facilities at the start of the new Millennium.* ***Left:*** *An aerial view of the College.* ***Below:*** *The Mons Hill Campus.*

Bent on winning

The arch is one of the most important and beautiful architectural innovations. The Romans are credited with its invention, and so durable did it turn out to be that examples of Roman arches are still to be seen all over the former Roman Empire more than 2000 years after they were built. The Romans of course built mainly in stone and brick, and whilst the shape of the arch survived for many decades, the construction materials used altered dramatically.

In 19th century Britain the material of choice was cast iron. Iron masters believed almost anything could be made from cast iron, from coffins to candlesticks. And of course they also gave us the cast iron arch, many of which can still be seen in Victorian buildings & bridges.

Cast iron arches appeared everywhere, from the roofs of the great railway termini to the Crystal Palace, built to house the Great Exhibition of 1851 and the largest fully-glazed building in the world at that time.

Above: Founder, Frank Barnshaw at work rolling and, inset, early premises at the old Arco site.
Below: An example of Victorian cast iron arches, now on display at the Black Country Living Museum in Dudley. The arches were from the Rolfe Street Baths building - originally in Smethwick, but now rebuilt at the museum as a tourist attraction and exhibition hall. Right: The impressive glazed vault at the Ealing Broadway Centre, London. The use of two types of joist bending were used to create this appearance, the centre arches in one semi-circular piece and the side arches in a hockey stick style.

Cast iron arches were manufactured by casting molten metal in the shape of a curve, however this process was very time-consuming. Wouldn't it be quicker to simply get a straight piece of iron and bend it into a curve? This is easier said than done. The problem with curving cast iron is that although it is very strong it is also very brittle; any attempt to bend cast iron results in it breaking. On the other hand steel (a carbon and iron alloy) is far more malleable and at the beginning of the 20th century steel began to take over from cast iron as a structural medium.

Basic steel bending is a simple process and is one of the foundation skills of Smithing, but that applies mainly to solid bars. For steel sections, even simple ones such as angles, it's

machinery and bending techniques and funded by a swing towards investment in public buildings.

Professional plumbers who want to bend a pipe use a pipe-bending tool. Similarly bending large steel sections and pipes into complex curves requires very sophisticated and powerful machinery. The specialised nature of the process and the high capital investment required means that it is unlikely that it would be economical for most companies to invest in this type of equipment. However help is a hand; The Angle Ring Company of Tipton uses custom built machinery and innovative techniques to tackle some of the biggest bending contracts in Europe.

To see how these techniques were developed we step back in time a little to 1951. Before today's curved structures were conceived steel was being curved for use in industry, and a number of 'section bending' companies offering rings made from light flat bar and angles were serving a thriving industrial sector.

At this time Frank Barnshaw founded 'Angle Ring' in Tipton. Before founding the business Frank had tried a number of enterprising ideas including making doll's prams and early supermarket trolleys which unfortunately proved unsuccessful. Frank had previously worked for a section-bending firm in the north of England and recognised a demand for this type of work in the heavily industrialised Midlands. He used those skills to launch 'Angle Ring' in Hurst Lane, Tipton.

At first the new firm was involved in the rolling of small angle and flat rings for ductwork flanges, vessel stiffeners

Top and left: Examples of cold rolling, an established metal bending technique. *Below:* An example of induction bending.

not quite as easy as that. Furthermore 'hollow' sections such as tubes and boxes and 'open' sections, such as joists, beams and channels are even more difficult to bend.

Anyone who has ever tried to bend a copper pipe for simple plumbing work soon discovers that unless one is very careful the pipe will suddenly collapse at the point of bending.

Whilst the economical cost of steel compared to cast iron made it the preferred structural medium the machinery and techniques for bending structural steel sections did not exist and so the 20th century seemed to herald the decline of the arch as a preferred architectural form. From the 1930s onwards a new brutalism began to occupy architectural minds. Squares and straight lines became the geometry of choice.

Over recent decades however the more natural line of the curve has increasingly begun to reappear. This has been driven by a demand for change from the regular shapes of concrete and straight steel frames and made possible by the development of modern

and other light engineering applications, at least when they were able to do so - simply obtaining steel for bending was quite difficult in the early years since steel was still being rationed following the war.

To begin with the business was hardly hi-tech, and rudimentary bending machinery was made by the founder himself using second hand lorry axles! These basic machines were utilised to bend a range of relatively small angle and flat bar sections, far removed from the full range of light, medium and heavy sections it would eventually become possible to curve.

Early working practices differ significantly from those of today. For instance Frank Barnshaw would regularly deliver rings to local clients himself by rolling them along the pavement by hand; on other occasions local traffic would come to a standstill when longer bars were carried into the main road to be checked for accuracy against a radius drawn on the tarmac!

The firm remained at its original premises in Hurst Lane for eleven years then in 1962 the company moved along the road to its present base in Bloomfield Road, Tipton. The new site would eventually expand from a single production unit to enclose an area of 18,000 square metres incorporating 15 production bays.

A major breakthrough occurred in the 1970s when Angle Ring developed machinery, tooling and techniques that enabled the curving of heavy beams, channels and columns about their major axes to radii previously deemed impossible.

Curving about the major axis poses several problems, the most significant of which is that the high loading required to induce the curve tends to cause the web of the section to buckle. The availability of heavy sections curved to previously unachievable radii gave architects and structural engineers far greater scope than ever before. This newly available range of products stimulated designers to incorporate many more curved elements into their buildings and structural designs.

Inevitably the company was repeatedly asked for sections bigger and stronger than the last, and having created a market for curved sections for structural purposes it became important to keep pace with that market. Since machines were not commercially available to accommodate such sections Angle Ring, still true to its founder's philosophy, designed and built them in-house. Once built these machines allowed the entire range of British and European sections to be curved.

*Above: The Poplar Walkway. **Right:** A trial bend for the Poplar high level walkway, London. **Below left:** Plate Rolling. **Below:** A Press Brake used to form and fold plate.*

The semi-circular barrel vault was however by no means the only application for Angle Ring's products. Curved structural sections opened up other possibilities - three and four centred arches, tudor arches, pointed arches along with other forms of vaulted construction such as fan, domed or sail vaulted roofs.

The potential of curved sections was not limited to roofs, arcades and canopies. They could also be used to create galleries, balconies, mezzanine floors or as individual members such as splayed columns and arched lintels similar to those used in the Lloyd Chambers which made use of curved sections to provide the structural frame to several elements of the building.

As the market developed non-circular curves were also requested. Until this point most curved items consisted of

The range of steel sections that Angle Ring are able to curve is huge, from simple shapes such as flat-profile metal bars to squares and rounds, tee-bars, channels, beams and joists. Tubes and pipes may also be curved in round, square, rectangular, elliptical or semi-elliptical profiles. It is also possible to curve each section type and serial size about different axes (for example a simple flat bar might be bent on either its side as a 'wedding ring' on or on its edge like a 'washer').

Top left: Western Morning news offices and printing facilities. *Top right:* TGV Station, Charles de Galle Airport, Paris. *Left:* Old Street roundabout in London which has two large 559-mm diameter tubes curved to a 17,200-mm radius, which support an advertising frame. *Below*: Sainsbury's Superstore, Plymouth, where 168-mm diameter tubes were curved to create a three dimensional surface.

Angle Ring has long been associated with innovative and high profile contracts. One of the first prestige contracts the company carried out was to provide the curved rails supporting the revolving restaurant at the top of London's Post Office Tower which opened in 1966.

During the early 1980s the availability of such a wide range of curved structural sections prompted designers to become even more adventurous and demanding. These years would see the completion of several award winning buildings using curved sections in barrel vault roofs. These included the Chester-Le-Street civic centre and Liverpool's Festival Hall Building, winner of the Structural Steel Design Award in 1984.

complete rings, segments of a circle, or a segment with one or two tangential straight pieces. Architects and designers began to ask for elliptical, parabolic and multi-radius curves which are far more difficult to produce, but can significantly reduce fabrication time and expense in certain circumstances.

By the close of the 1980s the entire range of steel sections could be curved to a variety of shapes, in any length, in any material grade. The desire by engineers to produce designs that were larger and more eye-catching than anything before created a new market. That market was for 'induction-bent' sections. The induction bending process involves heating a narrow band of material, bending it, cooling it and repeating the process for the next section of material. The process is slower than the traditional cold-bending method but it

allowed sections to be curved to radii far smaller than by cold bending. Induction bending had been used for many years in the production of tight-radius pipe bends for offshore and industrial applications but had not previously been utilised for sections or for structural applications.

During the early 1990s Angle Ring set about designing, building and installing a range of induction bending machines to allow tubes as large as 914 mm diameter to be curved. Using the wealth of bending experience gained during the previous forty years Angle Ring were able to incorporate several innovative features not normally associated with such machines, such as the ability to curve large hollow sections to very large radii. Commercially available machines of this type have a typical maximum radius of 10 or 15 metres; those built by Angle Ring have no such limitations.

Top: *Tube curved for the decorative Merchants Bridge in Manchester.* ***Left:*** *Rehabilitation of Overbridge, Airdrie.* ***Above:*** *Wimbledon No 1 court.*

The continuing challenge over the years has been sustaining the company's market position at the forefront of the industry and continually developing to meet customer requirements and expectations. As the firm continues into the new millennium Angle Ring has expanded its capabilities beyond tubes and sections and has diversified into other related steel bending areas. The acquisition of T Morley & Co of Birmingham allows the firm to undertake the bending of plates to form cylinders and tubes up to 200 mm thick including welding to Lloyds approved standards.

Angle Ring also has the capacity to manufacture bespoke closed profiles such as tubes or hollow sections, or open sections such as angles, channels and top-hat sections, all of which can be made to individual customer require-ments in most types of materials, including carbon, stainless steels and aluminium.

Looking toward the future there remains a seemingly insatiable desire by designers to be ever more adventurous. Having spent more than half a century ensuring that all steel leaving the factory was flat and not twisted the latest trend is for steel that has been intentionally curved in three dimensions!

Despite the many changes over the years the firm remains very much a family concern. Sadly, company founder Frank Barnshaw died in 1974 though not before getting a glimpse of what the future had in store for his company.

In the long run three generations of the Barnshaw family would work in the business - the founders' son Brian Barnshaw and later his sons Michael and Daniel.

Nor would the Barnshaws be the only family to be deeply involved with the firm. Ray Springthorpe had joined Frank Barnshaw as company manager and became Managing Director on Frank's death in 1974. Ray in turn retired in 1999 at which point his son David Springthorpe succeeded him as Managing Director.

Today the company's main markets are in structural and architectural metalwork, process and the oil and gas industry. Its aim is to continue to offer a competi-tive bending service of the highest quality and continue to set the standard for the rest of the industry to follow.

New demands, new challenges and new opportunities are the keynotes for the future, a future Angle Ring can face with confidence, building on the legacy of its inspiring past. And if those old Roman arches are looking a little shaky after two millennia then help is at hand. Angle Ring even specialise in bridge rehabilita-tion, manufacturing made to order, low-cost, curved steel sections to provide unobtrusive support underneath the original arch!

Top: *Part of the company fleet.*
Above left: *The latest development: curving of sections in three dimensions.*
Left: *A birds eye view of the Angle Ring site.*

Computing to work

To many of us it seems like computers only arrived in the world the day before yesterday. It may only have been in the 1990s that the home computer came of age and e-mails and the internet became part of our everyday lives but electronic computers have been around since the dark days of the second world war when they were first developed to help crack enemy codes.

Since the 1940s computers and computing power has grown at an extraordinary rate, their power doubling every 18 months, and what once seemed like (and indeed was) science fiction has become almost commonplace.

That development would not have happened without sufficient people trained in the use and development of computers to make the electronic revolution possible. One such firm which has done more than any other to train personnel to meet the challenge of the electronic age has been Dudley-based Computeach.

The company was founded in 1964 by 43 year old George Parkinson, then living in the midlands, though originally from Bolton in Greater Manchester.

Before the second world war Lancastrian George Parkinson had been an apprentice plumber until he was called up to serve in the Duke of Lancaster's Own Yeomanry and was posted to India.

Before leaving the army George Parkinson spent a period of

Top left: Founder George Parkinson. ***Above right:*** *George Parkinson pictured whilst serving in the Duke of Lancaster's Own Yeomanry in India.* ***Right:*** *Running the teashop in the early days.*

study at Exeter University to train as a lecturer for the Army Bureau of Current Affairs. That training introduced George to some of the fundamentals of distance learning - a methodology which was later to become the foundation on which the Computeach learning system would be built.

Following demobilisation George worked for himself, starting a number of enterprises including making steel frame greenhouses, running a teashop and going on the road selling refrigerators. Selling fridges led to the development of a new system of deep freeze construction which he marketed under the name of Scanfrost. George also worked as a site manager for Wimpey Homes where he reduced construction time using a technique called critical path analysis - an early form of systems analysis.

But fridges, greenhouses and house building were not what George really wanted; he believed that there was a great need and demand for high quality distance learning not least to learn about the exciting new technology of computers.

The times themselves were inspiring. These were the

the UK's very first independent computer training centre. The college soon moved on to premises alongside Chubb's in Lionel Street in the city - and by arrangement used Chubb's large IBM computer (at this time even the smallest computers were the size of an office suite and cost over £1 million) to give students hands-on training alongside their distance learning.

swinging sixties and the music of the time, epitomised by the Beatles, simply provided the soundtrack for a new optimism which was sweeping both Britain and the world after decades of austerity. The space race was on; no-one doubted that a man really would land on the moon before the end of the decade and anything seemed possible in Harold Wilson's 'white heat of technology'. The future was now! And at the forefront of that hi-tech future would be computers and those who knew how to use this remarkable new tool.

George Parkinson started the new business with very little capital and at first had to support it by going back on the road selling commercial toasting machines.

From a start up position of just five staff and 20 students George Parkinson pioneered a system of training now referred to as open or distance learning. Premises and student access to computers were rented, and a licence to reproduce course materials was negotiated with a Swiss gentleman. The courses were originally marketed under the name of Anglo Swiss.

The business opened from a suite of offices in Birmingham's Bullring Centre. The Computer Programming College was

Readers involved with computers in the early 1960s will recall just how much has changed since then: punched cards and punched tape were only just beginning to be challenged by the newer technology of magnetic tape, then stored on massive reels, whilst the idea of user friendly programs displayed on colourful screens was still years in the future. For most of the population 'programming' was still something to do with the BBC and 'networking' something fishermen might do. The thought that one day people would have in their own homes computers more powerful than the largest then constructed was sheer fantasy.

But for those with foresight computers were not fantasy but reality and represented the greatest opportunity for commercial development since the invention of the steam engine two centuries earlier which led to the Industrial Revolution.

George Parkinson was determined to be part of that new revolution. Meanwhile his wife Betty looked after the accounts and trusted

Top left: Scanfrost Coldrooms showroom.
Top right: Computeach Executives, 1967 (George Parkinson second left and former Dambuster pilot Bill Townsend far right).
Left: A 1940s computer.

colleagues, not least former Dambuster pilot Bill Townsend, helped George build up the business.

In the early days of Computeach the course materials consisted of training manuals complemented by live lectures on long-playing records, and research modules known as 'key ref,' a comprehension type search and learn process. Short bursts at ICL and IBM centres were also made available and the comprehensive training package, later universally known as open learning, was born.

In the early 1970s Computeach moved to Worcester Road, Hagley. In 1977 the company opened a London regional centre to handle a government contract to train the unemployed under the TOPS scheme. The London operation was based first in Drayton House, then Stephenson Way and ultimately Tennant Street before it closed in 1985.

From 1979 to 1984 Computeach's head office would be located in Metropolitan House in Fiveways Birmingham. In 1984 the head office moved from Hagley to Old Wharf Road in Stourbridge before moving to the current premises in Gornal in 1990 where Computeach remodelled the GWB Boilers site in Jews Lane to create University House.

Though the organisation has attempted exporting and to diversify into new markets over the years it would meet with limited success, but meanwhile the core business would grow steadily to become the UK's largest provider of computer training by distance learning.

In later years George would be helped in the business by his grandsons, Karl and Danny Parkinson.

Karl Parkinson started with Computeach in 1991 as a marketing assistant, moving on to become Special Projects Manager and later Development Director. Following the founder's death in 2001 he became the company's second chairman. Danny Parkinson, who had begun his career with Computeach in 1998, subsequently established the company's Multimedia department.

In 2001 Computeach was expanded by building a new purpose-built learning facility on the site - the aptly named Parkinson House.

Top right: *Computeach Open Learning Centre, 1984.*
Above right: *Collection of archived course materials and promotional material.* ***Far left:*** *George Parkinson celebrates Computeach's 25 years in computer training.* ***Left:*** *The GWB Boiler site in Jews Lane before remodelling by Computeach to create University House.*

of life who want to transfer from unrewarding jobs and train for a career in IT. Topics on offer include networking, website design, programming, systems analysis and database management.

Some of Computeach's students study whilst travelling the world, not least those serving in the armed forces, whilst the company has links with many British Consulates around the world enabling students to take examinations on their premises.

By the opening years of the third millennium Computeach had become the UK's largest provider of distance learning IT training in the UK, and had set the standard for high quality learning programmes with a first time pass rate for its students of over 80 per cent. Continuously developing the products it offers Computeach is ensuring that it will remain at the cutting edge of both technology and teaching for the foreseeable future.

The opening of Parkinson House by Her Royal Highness the Princess Royal on 25th October 2001 was an occasion that George Parkinson had organised to celebrate the success of Computeach. Her Royal Highness toured the facility meeting students past and present before unveiling a plaque and planting a tree in the grounds.

Today Computeach's approach is essentially the same as ever; only the materials and media have changed: students now learn via a 'blended learning solution', including interactive courseware downloaded from the internet or CD-ROM as well as traditional paper-based modules. These formats are combined with in-centre study days in Computeach's state of the art facilities in Gornal whilst at home tutorial support is provided via phone, fax, e-mail and of course post!

Computeach now offers some 17 different training combinations at both standard and advanced level, encompassing every IT discipline and taken up by individuals from all walks

Top left *The opening of Parkinson House by Her Royal Highness the Princess Royal in celebration of the success of Computeach, October 2001.*
Above left: *e-learning course materials, 2001.*
Right: *Chairman Karl Parkinson (seated) and his brother Danny Parkinson, grandsons of the founder George Parkinson.*
Below: *The existing Computeach site, Jews Lane, University House and new Parkinson House.*

The stamp of excellence

The Midlands contains a treasure trove of modest sized family firms whose provenance goes back generations to the days of Victorian England when a thousand factory chimney's pierced the local skies. Few businesses better illustrate the history of such firms as John Buckley (Dudley) Ltd with its premises just off King Street.

Having been born in 1853, the year the Crimean War began, no doubt John Buckley always felt at home in his office in Dudley's Alma Place, an address named after a battle in that now long distant war. And the company John founded is still there.

The firm was started by 30 year old John Buckley in 1883 and became a limited company in 1909. As well as owning a foundry in Church Street, John Buckley also owned the Royal Exchange pub next door at 13 Church Street; brewing and running the pub had been his occupation before opening the foundry.

In retrospect this seems an unusual move. Foundry work being a notoriously thirsty job one might have thought that a more likely move would be for a foundry owner to buy a pub rather than the other way round; but no doubt John Buckley was attracted to the new undertaking by close proximity of the foundry and, as a publican, by the close relationship he had inevitably already built up with local foundry workers.

John would often arrive in the foundry through the back door of his pub, having no doubt already slaked his own anticipated thirst on the way in.

If he was not already well known in Dudley John Buckley would soon come to be better known; though not as well known perhaps as the company dog, a wire-haired terrier owned by the founder who accompanied his master everywhere - except when he took it into his doggy head to travel on his own on the tram between Dudley and Netherton.

According to the trade directory of 1900 John Buckley describes himself as a malleable iron founder and range knob manufacturer for black leaded grates which are now only a distant memory. Well, a fairly distant memory, and though even the oldest of readers will have difficulty recalling new cast iron ovens being

Top: Founder, John Buckley.
Right: John Buckley pictured with the company dog who accompanied his master almost everywhere.

installed in homes many readers who are middle-aged will easily recall visiting houses as late as the 1960s and in a few cases into the 1970s, which still boasted such by then largely defunct kitchen features.

At the start of the 20th century however cast iron ovens and fireplaces were still very much in demand and as a consequence so were the various bits of 'furniture' to go with them such as knobs, handles and hinges.

In those days it was hard work making things in metal; the range knobs were made by Buckley's using Oliver or 'Tommy' hammers so-called after their inventor the engineer Thomas Oliver.

At the time of incorporation in 1909 the directors were John Buckley, Edward Russon, Ruth Rowe and Sarah Ann Russon. The two ladies were John Buckley's daughters whilst Edward Russon was the founder's son-in-law.

In 1910 a bad fire damaged the premises, part of which had to be rebuilt and about the same time the premises at 12 Alma Place, which are now the company offices,

were bought, and the office moved out of the pub. By now the foundry was employing some 25 men and a handful of boys.

During the first world war the company was making range knobs, fire irons (pokers and tongues and shovels) in iron with brass and copper heads; there was also a plating shop which used copper, brass and nickel as well as a casting shop in brass and copper.

At the end of the Great War, following the death of John Buckley in 1919, the demand for fire irons fell as Companion Stands were introduced. The production of range knobs and rivets however continued.

Edward Russon died in 1924. At that time the main products were still range knobs and rivets which the company supplied to the majority of foundries in England and Scotland as well as sending small quantities to Ireland and Australia.

Above: *Ruth Rowe (nee Buckley) a Director of the firm in 1919.* **Below:** *John Buckley, (extreme left) and employees, circa 1910.*

The company was by now also supplying cycle pedal pins for the Raleigh cycle company in Nottingham and steel bottom bracket axles to AJ Phillips of Smethwick.

The company's own main supplier of wrought iron at this time was Roberts & Cooper of Brettel Lane, Brierley Hill and steel from Round Oak Works.

In 1925, following Edward Russon's death, and with the next generation as yet still too young to take charge, a Mr J Phillips joined the business as company secretary and later became a director. During the next few years the company made steel pokers for Woolworth's supplying all its 700 stores right across the country.

Though the years immediately following the Great War had been good ones with the national economy doing well for a few years, nevertheless, there were ominous signs that good times were not going to last. Slowly the short-lived boom of the early 1920s began to go into reverse and in 1929 came the Wall Street crash which in turn drove the whole world into the great Depression which saw millions thrown on the dole. Many customers had difficulty paying their accounts.

That year Buckley's took over the business of H Townsend at Dudley which owed the firm money, along with a lot of other companies in Dudley, and began to make hearth furniture.

Sarah Russon had died in 1926 just two years after her husband; Ruth Rowe died in 1930. J Phillips was sacked in 1933 and John Edward Rowe, Ruth's son, who had joined the firm in 1924 at the age of 14, now became company secretary and a director having reached the age of 21. John Rowe would later recall that he was paid 12 shillings (60p) a week when he started, at a time when average wages paid in the works were between £3 and £3 10 shillings (£3.50) for a 40 hour week.

The trade in range knobs had declined during the 1920s and 1930s with the gradual introduction of gas and electric for heating and cooking. These were perhaps the most difficult times ever for the company, with trade poor everywhere, but most particularly in the products with which the company had made its name; but somehow Buckley's survived.

In 1938 the company built a stamp shop in Alma Place when all the houses there had been pulled down in a slum clearance scheme. That year Louis Hadley Rowe, now 21, joined his older brother John and began his working life in the new stamping shop. Tom Leighton had just started as shop manager in 1939 when war broke out and the company moved to making metal stampings for the war effort.

Above: *Brothers John Edward Rowe (left) and Louis Hadley Rowe.*

Stampings were produced for Rolls Royce at Derby, components which were destined to become part of Spitfire engines, and parts for many other firms in the Birmingham area making war materials. One of the largest customers however was for the curiously named Wolsey Sheep Shearing Company of Witton, making the central plugs of the 10lbs practice bombs of which some 5,000 were produced every week.

Buckley's now also made stampings in 'Duraluminium' for Dunlop of Coventry who made aircraft components. During the war years Buckley's own major suppliers were firms such as ICI Witton, EP Jenks of Wolverhampton, McKechnie Bros. of Birmingham and Manganese Bronze Ltd in Ipswich.

At the close of hostilities the company quickly returned to producing all kinds of general commercial parts, a long term strategy which would ensure the firm's continuance to the present day.

The founder's great grandson Tim Rowe would join the firm in 1965 and his son in turn, Tim Rowe junior, would begin helping his father in 1996 following the deaths of Louis Rowe in 1981 and John Edward Rowe in 1992.

Since being founded by local publican and brewer John Buckley his company has happily remained a family firm. In the years since 1938 when the company began making brass stampings it has supplied over 2,500 different patterns to all types of businesses, not only to Rolls Royce, Raleigh and Woolworth's but so many other well known names such as Jaguar and Laura Ashley.

Today the company's 20 or so employees use power presses to make stampings for hydraulic components, pneumatic applications, lock assemblies, architectural furniture, fancy goods and parts for the motor and water industries in addition to many other trades.

*Above: A sample of components manufactured by the company. **Below:** The present day staff of John Buckley (Dudley) Ltd.*

Homes of our own

An Englishman's home is his castle. And though not everyone can own a castle, everyone would like to own their own home. That is particularly true in Dudley and it was just as true nearly a century and half ago when the Dudley Building Society was born.

The Dudley and District Benefit Building Society was founded in 1858 with the principle aim of enabling working men to buy their own homes. The Society's first premises were opposite the Wesley Chapel in Wolverhampton Street.

The times were however not particularly favourable for launching such an enterprise since the period was one of a general depression in trade. Even so at the end of the first year of operations the Society had acquired 64 members and received some £574 as deposits of which £330 had been loaned out as mortgages.

In 1865 the Society moved to premises at 195 High Street, and 13 years later to 224 Market Place where it would remain until moving to its present offices at Dudley House in Stone Street in 1963.

At the outset investors were asked to buy shares worth between £30 and £120 to be paid for by

Top: Senior Secretary Mr TW Tanfield (seated) discusses a mortgage application with Joint Secretary Mr AR Tanfield in 1935.
Below: Boardroom at 224 Market Street, Dudley.
Right: Offices on the first floor of 224 Market Street, Dudley, the site of the Society's Head Office from 1893-1996.

subscriptions of between 2s 6d (12.5p) and 7 1/2d (3p) per week. Investors were promised 5 per cent compound interest per annum, whilst borrowers were encouraged to take loans to buy property on land to erect houses and factories and to pay off existing mortgages. Simple interest only was charged to borrowers at the rate of 5 per cent on the balance of any money owing at the end of each year.

The formula was a success. By the time of the first world war over a million pounds had passed through the Society. Councillor TW Tanfield, who by then had been connected with the Building Society for 24 years, and was now its Secretary had helped direct much of that money to helping develop the estates at Blower's Green, Scot's Green and other local places resulting in hundreds of new homes being built in Dudley.

On the outbreak of the Great War in 1914 after 56 years of its existence the Society's Secretary TW Tanfield was able to

In 1996 Dudley Building Society became a tied Agent of Legal and General and offered additional services to its customers who required wider advice on financial service matters. Following mortgage regulation in 2001 the Society could no longer remain as a tied Agent and created a subsidiary known as Dudley Financial Services Limited, which now forms part of the Dudley Group. Today the Group has five branch offices around Dudley as well as an equal number of agents in the Midlands and Wales, offering a comprehensive range of financial services including mortgages, savings and insurance.

By the first year of the new millennium the Society's assets had grown from that small start back in 1858 to over £130 million.

report that despite a number of unplanned withdrawals by men rushing off to serve at the front the Society's assets had now reached £208,000, an increase of £7,130 over the previous year despite the rush of withdrawals.

The Annual Report for the year 1915 quaintly records that two members of the Society had died in the previous twelve months one having been 'called away' the other 'summoned hence'.

By 1919 however the death of a director was reported as simply that - a death: the war to end wars had changed attitudes and our language. It had also changed the Society's fortunes with assets having risen to £266,000. With a reserve fund of £14,037 in hand the directors had no hesitation in agreeing to contribute £500 to the Dudley 'Peace Memorial' Fund.

Though the years between the wars were harsh ones, buying ones own house was still proving popular - perhaps not surprising when interest rates were very low indeed - and they would fall even lower. In 1940 the first full year of the second world war, by which time assets had reached £1,279,959, the Society cut its rate to borrowers from 3 per cent to just 2.5 per cent, surely a major incentive to buy if there ever was one.

The Society is constantly giving support to the local community. The Society has developed special mortgage facilities to provide assistance to individuals with special needs. It also works closely with five local Primary Schools to encourage savings at an early age, as well as operating a Save and Sponsor Savings Account that provides financial support to the local Mary Stevens Hospice derived from the balances held.

'The Dudley' was however still true to its founding principles, remaining an independent mutual building society despite efforts to persuade it to do otherwise. And though it may not be the biggest Building Society in the world it does still aim to be the best.

Top left: Officers and cadets from the Dudley Sea Cadet Unit 'TS Centaur' celebrate the donation of a cheque presented by General Manager and Secretary KE Robinson on behalf of the Society. Left: Former Chief Executive Alan Johnson (left) pictured with Superintendent Gary Cann and Dudley MP Ross Cranston at the launch of 'Cameras for the Elderly' as a crime prevention campaign. Above: Society employee Meg Pottinger presents Tomas Adams of Oakham Primary School with a book voucher in July 2001 to mark his achievements of saving £1,000 with the Society.

To Market to Market

There's one thing for sure, even if you've lived in Dudley all your life, you will have visited the Dudley market in your childhood. The market has been there for a very long time indeed and who can ever forget as a child being taken around from stall to stall clinging to mother's skirts amongst the throng of folk keen to stock up on fresh fruit and vegetables, or search for a pair of cheap plimsolls for PE?

Markets are special, they are full of life in a way that the sanitised shops of national chains can never compete with. The sounds of vendors shouting their wares and the smells of fresh produce in the market linger ineradicably down the years.

It is believed that the market at Dudley goes back to the late 12th century and first came into being shortly after the civil war known as 'The Anarchy' which was fought between supporters of King Stephen and the Empress Matilda in the 1130s and 40s. The earliest documentation of the market however is dated 1230.

The market place, which was then located in exactly the same place as it is today, was initially controlled by the Earl of Dudley but was later taken over by the Priory.

Weekly markets and annual fairs were organised by the Priory; special market days included cattle, cheese and stock sales in March, lamb in August and cheese and onion in September.

Both market place and market have undergone many changes over the years. It was not until the early 14th century that the High Street and Market Place were paved,

Right: *Market Stallholders pictured in 1895.*
Below: *A 19th century artists impression of Dudley Market.*

More recently, in 1998/99, the whole market was completely refurbished. The old canvas roof was taken down and the metal stalls re-roofed with asphalt tiles giving the whole market a new, modern appearance. The Old Market Place paving stones were replaced with modern block paving and the lighting on the stalls upgraded, each one now having twin fluorescent tubes and mains power.

Today Dudley Market consists of 74 fixed stalls and one mobile unit and opens on six days each week from 8 am to 5.30 pm. Of the 85 traders who have stalls at Dudley nine are there every day whilst the remainder average three days at Dudley enabling them to open at other markets in the area on the other days.

improving access for the public and making conditions for traders so much better.

Though the town of Dudley would grow significantly over the years its market has remained conveniently located in the very centre of town, though now in a pedestrianised precinct.

In the early 1980s the market consisted of a wooden framework supporting a canvas roof with wooden trestle tables used as stalls. The wooden framework was replaced in 1982/3 with tubular metal and a new canvas roof was fitted.

At the start of the 1990s the centre of Dudley, and especially its market, suffered a severe setback; the management of most of the town's major high street stores including British Home Stores, Marks and Spencers, C&A and Littlewoods all made a decision to pull out of the town centre and relocate some four miles away to the then new Merry Hill Centre. Initially this had a disastrous effect on town centre trade with visitor numbers dramatically reduced. Fortunately the downturn did not last too long and, helped by several marketing campaigns to promote the town centre and the market, by the end of the decade it was business as usual.

Around ten casual traders can usually be accommodated each day, providing they arrive before 8.30 am and they get treated on a first come first served basis. Access for shoppers is excellent with ten car parks all within easy walking distance of the market as well as some on-street car parking near by. The site is kept spotlessly clean with cleaning being carried out throughout the day by the Borough Council.

The regular traders, some of whom have been at the market for four generations, are a happy bunch who work well together and are all prepared to help each other. At the start of the 21st century these descendants of Medieval traders are still enjoying the benefits of a market which is almost 900 years old.

Top left: *Dudley Market pictured in the early 1970s.* ***Above left:*** *A bustling Market in the 1950s.* ***Left:*** *Shoppers still enjoying the benefits of Dudley Market in 2002.*

Hot stuff

One of the oldest conundrums around is 'in what can you store a universal solvent'? A more practical question, and one long familiar to those involved in smelting metal, is how to keep molten metal in a container which does not itself melt due to the high temperatures involved?

The answer to that tricky question is to use 'refractories' - materials which are used to line furnaces and which are capable of not only resisting very high temperatures without melting, but also great variations in temperature whilst at the same time not reacting chemically with the molten metals and gases in contact with them.

Refractory clay, and refractory cement containing a high percentage of alumina, have been used as refractories for a very long time and continue to be so - albeit now, in the 21st century, the science and technology applied to both materials and production ensure a far superior and reliable product than was known to our forefathers.

Robert Lickley Holdings Ltd is a privately owned independent group of companies engaged in the design, manufacture and supply of refractory products and associated furnace and kiln equipment.

The original Robert Lickley Ltd was formed in July 1970 and operated from a small factory unit in Oakengates, Shropshire, where the production of a specialised range of high quality fused alumina products was undertaken.

Company founder, Robert Lickley, had previously been Sales Director for Gibbons Refractories Ltd in Dudley before branching out on his own.

The philosophy of quality was uppermost in Robert's thinking even in those early days, with production facilities being designed to accommodate the mixing of 'castables' and cements in batches of such size as to ensure the consistency of the finished product on a bag for bag basis.

The success of that philosophy led to a considerable expansion of the company both in terms of its customer base and product

Top left: *Robert Lickley, founder of the company.*
Below: *Robert Lickley Refractories in the 1970s.*

two departments for producing pre-cast shapes which incorporate three mixers, a vibration table and three drying ovens.

A considerable amount of investment has been made in order to provide a fully equipped production facility inclusive of mould making using the very latest mixing and vibration equipment to ensure that ideal process conditions are met and quality maintained.

Such investment would include fully automated and calibrated drying ovens enabling the company to pre-dry the pre-cast shapes to a uniform consistency before delivery enabling customers to put them to immediate use.

Despite the challenge posed by three major recessions including the three day week, a three month steel strike in the 1980s and significant changes in castable refractory technology each obstacle to progress has in turn been overcome. Today main markets for Lickley products are the steel industry and non-ferrous metal production in the UK, together with similar outlets abroad.

Still a wholly independent firm at the start of the 21st century Robert Lickley Refractories Ltd aims to continue to be the UK's No. 1 independent manufacturer of high quality refractory castable and pre-cast products and to continue to ensure that the Robert Lickley name along with that of the company's Arelcrete and Arelset brand names retain their well earned national and international reputation.

range to the point where, after just 12 months, it became necessary to move to larger premises in Cradley Heath before buying freehold premises on the Dormston Trading Estate in Dudley's Burton Road in 1977.

The company was also involved with the design, supply, and in some cases the installation, of complete refectory linings both in the UK and overseas. Because of the diverse nature of the firm's business activities a decision was taken in 1977 to set up a holding company with subsidiaries, each of which would be responsible for its own specialised areas.

Robert Lickley would became a major figure in the industry in which he worked not only founding the company which bears his name but also becoming the founder member of the Institute of Refractory Engineers.

Since its foundation the company Robert Lickley has grown from a tiny operation using a single small batch mixer in which to mix refractory aggregate and high alumina cement, to one which operates two castable semi-automated mixer plants, a wet cement mixer plant, a semi-dry ramming mixing plant and

Top left: *The new modern Castable Mixing Plant.*
Above left: *Robert Lickley pictured with staff.*
Below: *Board of Directors.*

Britannia in the bath

How many readers can recall bathing in a tin bath in front of the fire? Of course though we called them 'tin' baths but really they were made from sheets of steel, 'galvanised' to prevent the steel from rusting by dipping the sheets in molten zinc to provide a protective coating. The uses of galvanised steel have been, and remain, uncountable ranging from corrugated roofing to those once innumerable tin baths.

There are not too many of us real oldsters left these days but there was a time that sometimes seems not too long ago when a tin bath, hung on a hook in the back yard when it was not in use, was what an awful lot of us took our weekly baths in. You have to go back quite a way now to remember mother bringing in the bath from its hook and putting it in front of the coal fire before filling it with it water from the stove; each child would take it in turns to bathe, with the last of all getting the dirtiest water.

With indoor plumbing becoming almost universal in the 1960s the old tin bath tub gradually disappeared, along with such other period pieces as the galvanised dustbin replaced by wheelie bins, paper bags and other novelties once hot ashes from coal fires were no longer likely to find their way into them.

It's perhaps surprising then to find that it is still perfectly possible to buy tin baths and galvanised dustbins. And even more surprising to find that the firm which makes them is a thriving modern business.

At the Britannia Works in Talbots Lane, Brierley Hill the family firm of H&E Knowles (Lye) Ltd is still turning out its famed Britannia brand traditional galvanised 'tin' baths and bins alongside dozens of other increasingly popular products.

Top left: Founder, Jack Knowles.
Above right: Eric Knowles at work.
Right: The production of dustbins in the early days. *Below:* The company's original tin bath.

By the 1990s the Britannia range of traditional products would include garden incinerators, wheelbarrows, cold frames and patio planters, greenhouse shelving, buckets and shovels, mop buckets, coal bunkers, plaster skips and watering cans. And of course the ever faithful dustbins and tin baths were still being made from galvanised sheets of metal, still to time honoured designs, even if the hammers and hand 'pressers' of the early days have long since been replaced by 500 tonne mechanised 'pressers' and 'formers'.

H&E Knowles was founded in the early 1920s by Jack Knowles. The company pioneered the manufacture of tin baths at its Lye works until the onset of the second world war.

Following the war Jack Knowles, along with his daughter and four sons, resumed production making tin baths and other galvanised wares, selling them in and around the Black Country.

In 1959 Jack's son Henry and his wife Ethel took control of the expanding business. Joined by their son Eric, Henry and Ethel began trading as H&E Knowles & Son.

Today's company H&E Knowles (Lye) Ltd was incorporated in 1962 and continues the family tradition of making quality galvanised wares. Henry Knowles died in the late 1960s following which, his widow Ethel and son Eric continued to build up the business.

Eric and his wife Alice would later expand the business even further with the introduction of new machinery and extending the product range.

When Eric and Alice's sons Peter and Paul joined the company as apprentices in the mid 1970s they started on the shop floor, eventually gaining a full working knowledge of every aspect of the business by working in all the divisions of the company.

Over the decades the company has survived the vicissitudes of fashion to see off all its main competitors. Its traditionally made British products have enjoyed a remarkable longevity and are now to be found in all major garden equipment retailers.

Today Peter Knowles is the fourth generation of the family to be at the helm of the business and is driving the company forward with new products and a world-wide export programme whilst continuing to bear in mind his mother's sage advice 'look after your employees and they will look after you'.

Peter's son Daniel has become the fifth generation of the family to join the company and expects to be soon joined by his sister Faith Knowles.

Top left: *Son of the founder Henry Knowles (known as Harry) and wife Ethel.* **Top right**: *Eric Knowles and wife Alice.* **Above left:** *Paul Knowles.* **Right:** *Managing Director Peter Knowles and his son Daniel.*

Building better pubs

Robert 'Bob' Bennett, a carpenter, started his own company on 1st June 1945 carrying out maintenance work in tied pubs for a local brewery. Bob Bennett had many contacts from his previous employer, a building company which had specialised in pub maintenance work but which went bankrupt. Bob used his contacts to forge the beginning of a business relationship which is continued by his firm to this day.

Bob originally ran the business from 13 Jews lane, Upper Gornal where he was helped by his wife Alice and daughter Joan. There in Jews Lane, in 1947, Bob was joined by Granville Wright who by then had married Joan.

Granville would become the Works Manager whilst Alice and Joan did the accounts.

The company grew and in 1948 moved into larger premises at 37 Jews Lane. The company then began carrying out small alterations to public houses in addition to basic maintenance.

Top left: *Founder, Robert (Bob) Bennett.*
Right: *The company's first lorry.*
Below: *Bennett's haulage yard in Jews Lane, 1954.*

Originally mainly hand tools were used. The firm's first circular saw was bought in 1951 and over the years more and more machinery would be acquired which would eventually result in an impressive joinery shop.

In the meantime however R Bennett & Co Ltd was acquiring an excellent reputation in its niche market for maintaining and altering public houses and again outgrew its premises.

In 1954 the company bought a haulage yard in Jews Lane which had not only yard and buildings but also a building to house the joinery shop.

The new premises were gradually extended and altered increasing the amount of available work space as the firm invested in more joinery machinery to allow it to expand even more and carry out ever larger contracts. As the business grew Tim Wright, Granville's son joined the company in 1967; Tim would eventually become Managing Director whilst his wife Joy did the wages and accounts.

Bob Bennett retired in 1968 and shortly

to the brewing industry and has worked for many local and national companies offering maintenance, alterations and new build projects costing up to £1 million. The firm has also expanded into the retail trade and has worked abroad fitting out public houses in Europe.

The company's business philosophy is to provide a friendly professional service which can quickly respond to customers' needs. In keeping with that philosophy the firm believes in recruiting and training its own operatives and over the years has had had no fewer than 17 members of staff who have each clocked up over 25 years service with the company and one who managed 50 years!

Such long service has ensured that the company has always maintained a high degree of skill and craftsmanship to call upon. That reservoir of skill backed up by more than half a century of knowledge has enabled the company to provide a consistently reliable and high quality service and to continuously build on its solid reputation for meeting customers' requirements.

The future of the firm lies with continued and controlled development through maintaining a dedicated workforce, investment and ensuring quality of the end product - and above all teamwork. That future looks bright with Tim and Joy's children Jennie and David Wright now having joined the company as respectively, Office Manager and Trainee Surveyor, to continue the family line in this quintessential family business.

afterwards Bob Croxford, who would eventually become a director, joined the company. Sadly Granville Wright died in September 1974 just as George Rudge, who would also subsequently become a director joined, the firm.

Despite the loss of Granville Wright and the retirement of its founder the business nevertheless continued to expand and in 1977 moved to its present premises at Constitution Hill, Dudley.

In 1979 and 1983 further parcels of land were acquired to add to the original purchase. The original joinery shop was demolished in 1984 and replaced by a new building which was in its turn extended in 1989.

The original office block was extended in 1986 and 1995 - and totally rebuilt in 2000 to keep pace with expansion. True to its traditions the company continued to reinvest profits to allow for controlled growth.

R Bennett & Co Ltd had by now become a specialist company providing a complete service

Top left: *Jews Lane, 1976.*
Above left: *A public house fitted out by Bennett's.*
Below: *The company Headquarters.*

Families enjoying a day out at Dudley Zoo in 1957.

Acknowledgments

The publishers would like to thank

Sam Robbins and Hilary Atkins - Dudley Metropolitan Borough Council

Archives & Local History Service

Andrew Mitchell

Steve Ainsworth

True North Books Ltd - Book List

Memories of Accrington - 1 903204 05 4

Memories of Barnet - 1 903204 16 X

Memories of Barnsley - 1 900463 11 3

Golden Years of Barnsley -1 900463 87 3

Memories of Basingstoke - 1 903204 26 7

Memories of Bedford - 1 900463 83 0

More Memories of Bedford - 1 903204 33 X

Golden Years of Birmingham - 1 900463 04 0

Birmingham Memories - 1 903204 45 3

Memories of Blackburn - 1 900463 40 7

More Memories of Blackburn - 1 900463 96 2

Memories of Blackpool - 1 900463 21 0

Memories of Bolton - 1 900463 45 8

More Memories of Bolton - 1 900463 13 X

Bolton Memories - 1 903204 37 2

Memories of Bournemouth -1 900463 44 X

Memories of Bradford - 1 900463 00 8

More Memories of Bradford - 1 900463 16 4

More Memories of Bradford II - 1 900463 63 6

Bradford Memories - 1 903204 47 X

Bradford City Memories - 1 900463 57 1

Memories of Bristol - 1 900463 78 4

More Memories of Bristol - 1 903204 43 7

Memories of Bromley - 1 903204 21 6

Memories of Burnley - 1 900463 95 4

Golden Years of Burnley - 1 900463 67 9

Memories of Bury - 1 900463 90 3

Memories of Cambridge - 1 900463 88 1

Memories of Cardiff - 1 900463 14 8

Memories of Carlisle - 1 900463 38 5

Memories of Chelmsford - 1 903204 29 1

Memories of Cheltenham - 1 903204 17 8

Memories of Chester - 1 900463 46 6

More Memories of Chester -1 903204 02 X

Memories of Chesterfield -1 900463 61 X

More Memories of Chesterfield - 1 903204 28 3

Memories of Colchester - 1 900463 74 1

Nostalgic Coventry - 1 900463 58 X

Coventry Memories - 1 903204 38 0

Memories of Croydon - 1 900463 19 9

More Memories of Croydon - 1 903204 35 6

Golden Years of Darlington - 1 900463 72 5

Nostalgic Darlington - 1 900463 31 8

Darlington Memories - 1 903204 46 1

Memories of Derby - 1 900463 37 7

More Memories of Derby - 1 903204 20 8

Memories of Dewsbury & Batley - 1 900463 80 6

Memories of Doncaster - 1 900463 36 9

Nostalgic Dudley - 1 900463 03 2

Golden Years of Dudley - 1 903204 60 7

Memories of Edinburgh - 1 900463 33 4

Memories of Enfield - 1 903204 14 3

Memories of Exeter - 1 900463 94 6

Memories of Glasgow - 1 900463 68 7

More Memories of Glasgow - 1 903204 44 5

Memories of Gloucester - 1 903204 04 6

Memories of Grimsby - 1 900463 97 0

More Memories of Grimsby - 1 903204 36 4

Memories of Guildford - 1 903204 22 4

Memories of Halifax - 1 900463 05 9

More Memories of Halifax - 1 900463 06 7

Golden Years of Halifax - 1 900463 62 8

Nostalgic Halifax - 1 903204 30 5

Memories of Harrogate - 1 903204 01 1

Memories of Hartlepool - 1 900463 42 3

Memories of High Wycombe - 1 900463 84 9

Memories of Huddersfield - 1 900463 15 6

More Memories of Huddersfield - 1 900463 26 1

Golden Years of Huddersfield - 1 900463 77 6

Nostalgic Huddersfield - 1 903204 19 4

Huddersfield Town FC - 1 900463 51 2

Memories of Hull - 1 900463 86 5

More Memories of Hull - 1 903204 06 2

Memories of Ipswich - 1 900463 09 1

More Memories of Ipswich - 1 903204 52 6

Memories of Keighley - 1 900463 01 6

Golden Years of Keighley - 1 900463 92 X

Memories of Kingston - 1 903204 24 0

Continued overleaf

True North Books Ltd - Book List

Memories of Leeds - 1 900463 75 X

More Memories of Leeds - 1 900463 12 1

Golden Years of Leeds - 1 903204 07 0

Memories of Leicester - 1 900463 08 3

More Memories of Leicester - 1 903204 08 9

Memories of Leigh - 1 903204 27 5

Memories of Lincoln - 1 900463 43 1

Memories of Liverpool - 1 900463 07 5

More Memories of Liverpool - 1 903204 09 7

Liverpool Memories - 1 903204 53 4

Memories of Luton - 1 900463 93 8

Memories of Macclesfield - 1 900463 28 8

Memories of Manchester - 1 900463 27 X

More Memories of Manchester - 1 903204 03 8

Manchester Memories - 1 903204 54 2

Memories of Middlesbrough - 1 900463 56 3

More Memories of Middlesbrough - 1 903204 42 9

Memories of Newbury - 1 900463 79 2

Memories of Newcastle - 1 900463 81 4

More Memories of Newcastle - 1 903204 10 0

Memories of Newport - 1 900463 59 8

Memories of Northampton - 1 900463 48 2

More Memories of Northampton - 1 903204 34 8

Memories of Norwich - 1 900463 73 3

Memories of Nottingham - 1 900463 91 1

More Memories of Nottingham - 1 903204 11 9

Bygone Oldham - 1 900463 25 3

Memories of Oldham - 1 900463 76 8

Memories of Oxford - 1 900463 54 7

Memories of Peterborough - 1 900463 98 9

Golden Years of Poole - 1 900463 69 5

Memories of Portsmouth - 1 900463 39 3

More Memories of Portsmouth - 1 903204 51 8

Nostalgic Preston - 1 900463 50 4

More Memories of Preston - 1 900463 17 2

Preston Memories - 1 903204 41 0

Memories of Reading - 1 900463 49 0

Memories of Rochdale - 1 900463 60 1

More Memories of Reading - 1 903204 39 9

More Memories of Rochdale - 1 900463 22 9

Memories of Romford - 1 903204 40 2

Memories of St Albans - 1 903204 23 2

Memories of St Helens - 1 900463 52 0

Memories of Sheffield - 1 900463 20 2

More Memories of Sheffield - 1 900463 32 6

Golden Years of Sheffield - 1 903204 13 5

Memories of Slough - 1 900 463 29 6

Golden Years of Solihull - 1 903204 55 0

Memories of Southampton - 1 900463 34 2

More Memories of Southampton - 1 903204 49 6

Memories of Stockport - 1 900463 55 5

More Memories of Stockport - 1 903204 18 6

Memories of Stockton - 1 900463 41 5

Memories of Stoke-on-Trent - 1 900463 47 4

More Memories of Stoke-on-Trent - 1 903204 12 7

Memories of Stourbridge - 1903204 31 3

Memories of Sunderland - 1 900463 71 7

More Memories of Sunderland - 1 903204 48 8

Memories of Swindon - 1 903204 00 3

Memories of Uxbridge - 1 900463 64 4

Memories of Wakefield - 1 900463 65 2

More Memories of Wakefield - 1 900463 89 X

Nostalgic Walsall - 1 900463 18 0

Golden Years of Walsall - 1 903204 56 9

More Memories of Warrington - 1 900463 02 4

Memories of Watford - 1 900463 24 5

Golden Years of West Bromwich - 1 900463 99 7

Memories of Wigan - 1 900463 85 7

Golden Years of Wigan - 1 900463 82 2

Nostalgic Wirral - 1 903204 15 1

Memories of Woking - 1 903204 32 1

Nostalgic Wolverhampton - 1 900463 53 9

Wolverhampton Memories - 1 903204 50 X

Memories of Worcester - 1 903204 25 9

Memories of Wrexham - 1 900463 23 7

Memories of York - 1 900463 66 0